MENTAL ILLNESS IN THE UNITED STATES

MENTAL ILLNESS IN THE UNITED STATES

Epidemiological Estimates

- Bruce P. Dohrenwend
- Barbara Snell Dohrenwend
- Madelyn Schwartz Gould
- Bruce Link
- Richard Neugebauer
- Robin Wunsch-Hitzig

PRAEGER

PRAEGER SPECIAL STUDIES • PRAEGER SCIENTIFIC

Library of Congress Cataloging in Publication Data

Main entry under title:

Mental illness in the United States.

    Includes bibliographical references and index.
    1. Mental illness--United States. 2. Mental
illness--United States--Statistics. 3. United States
--Statistics, Medical. I. Dohrenwend, Bruce Philip,
1927-   [DNLM: 1. Mental disorders--Occurrence--
United States. WM100.3 M549]
RC443.M46   614.5'8'0973   79-18725
ISBN 0-03-053506-9

Published in 1980 by Praeger Publishers
CBS Educational and Professional Publishing
A Division of CBS, Inc.
521 Fifth Avenue, New York, New York 10017 U.S.A.

© 1980 by Praeger Publishers

123456789   038   98765432

Printed in the United States of America

PREFACE

The President's Commission on Mental Health was formed on February 17, 1977. Its purpose was to "review the mental health needs of the Nation and to make recommendations to the President as to how the Nation might best meet these needs" (President's Commission on Mental Health, Vol. 1, 1978, p. 1). To assist the commission some 35 task panels of experts on various matters related to mental health were established. This book is based on a special working report that we prepared for one of these task panels, the Panel on Nature and Scope of the Problems.

Our special working report contained a series of analyses of the results of epidemiologic studies of true prevalence that we agreed to undertake in October 1977 at the request of Beatrix A. Hamburg, Commission Director of Studies. It was submitted on January 13, 1978 to the task panel. Although it contained some of the analyses we had hoped to provide, we could not complete several additional analyses in time for the final task panel report submitted in February 1978. Specifically, additional analyses of epidemiologic studies of childhood disorders had to be omitted as did a barely begun section on psychiatric disorders of the aged. Moreover, our work on relations between untreated and treated rates of various types of disorders was not as far along as we would have liked, and this was true as well of our investigation of studies using measures of what, following Jerome Frank's concept, we call "demoralization."

Since February 1978, we have been able to complete these additional analyses and, indeed, expand some of the previous analyses. The additions do not alter in any major way the results of our work that were included in the report to the President's Commission on Mental Health. The full analyses presented here do, however, extend the earlier findings as well as clarify the bases on which they rest. Moreover, we have attempted to spell out in greater detail our own views as to how firm these findings are and their main implications both for further research and for the planning and evaluation of mental health services.

The analyses included in this volume represent a collaborative effort with Barbara Snell Dohrenwend and with the following group of predoctoral and postdoctoral fellows in the National Institute of Mental Health (NIMH) supported (MH 13043) Research Training Program in Psychiatric Epidemiology at Columbia University—Madelyn Schwartz Gould, Bruce G. Link, Richard Neugebauer, and Robin Wunsch—who are our coauthors. The division of labor among us is reflected in the listing of chapter authors in the Contents list. In addition, Barbara Dohrenwend did the final editing of the manuscript prior to its submission for publication.

We would like to thank our fellow members of the Task Panel on the Nature and Scope of the Problems: Donald Cohen, Ruth Diggs, Barry Gurland, Morton Kramer, David Mechanic, Gloria Powell, Lee Robins, Robin Room, Lisbeth Schorr, Robert Spitzer, John Strauss, Myrna Weissman, and Helen Wright. They contributed valuable memoranda, comments, and criticisms that influenced us in developing this volume. However, we are responsible for the analyses and conclusions presented.

A number of colleagues who were not members of the task panel provided valuable advice and criticism on various parts of the book. They are Peter Cross, Sheppard Kellam, Robert Lubin, Judith Rabkin, Michael Rutter, David Shaffer, Patrick Shrout, and Samuel Toussie.

In addition, there is a group of people without whose extraordinarily generous help whole sections of this volume could not have been undertaken. These individuals provided us sometimes with tapes of their original data, sometimes with tables from their unpublished studies, and sometimes with special tabulations of data from archival sources on which they were working that contained unpublished information relevant to our needs. It is a special pleasure to be able to thank them publicly. They are Haroutun Babigian, Daniel Edwards, Wilbert Edgerton, Per Fugelli, Baqar Husaini, Daniel Mueller, Jerome Myers, James Neff, Eleanor Singer, George Warheit, and Myrna Weissman. We are most grateful.

Finally, we are grateful for financial support from the President's Commission on Mental Health. This unusual aid would not have been available without the strong advocacy of Beatrix Hamburg. It made it possible for the group of fellows in the Psychiatric Epidemiology Training Program to take time off from other activities and develop data analyses on an intensive basis over the very short period available to us for preparation of the special working report. These analyses were facilitated by valuable research assistance from Martha Tam, and Hannah Frisch did a marvelous job in typing the entire draft of the manuscript in the final form submitted to the publisher. The research was also supported in part by training grant MH 13043, research grant MH 10328, and Research Scientist Award KO5 MH 14663 from the NIMH, U.S. Public Health Service, and by the Foundations' Fund for Research in Psychiatry.

CONTENTS

LIST OF TABLES

LIST OF FIGURES

MENTAL ILLNESS IN THE UNITED STATES

1

INTRODUCTION

Bruce P. Dohrenwend

The charge from the President's Commission on Mental Health to the members of the Task Panel on the Nature and Scope of the Problems was as follows:

> Accurate estimates of the burden of illness and appreciation of the realistic potential for prevention have significant bearing on the allocation of resources for research, services and training of appropriate manpower to help ease the illness burden in future years.
>
> In order to promote mental health effectively and to treat or cure existing mental illness, it is necessary to have knowledge of the full range and magnitude of serious psychological disorder in the population. It will be the task of this group to report figures for the incidence and prevalance of overt mental illness in the total population. It will also be useful to report some comparative figures for socially significant sub-sets of the population, for example, in relation to socioeconomic status, age, sex, etc.
>
> It will also be the task of this panel to describe the distribution in the population of serious neurotic behavior, developmental or learning disabilities, psychophysiological disorders and serious problems of substance abuse. Trends over time in these areas would be useful.
>
> Ultimately, greatest gains in mental health should, in principle, come through prevention. Effective preventive intervention depends on recognition of the antecedents of mental disorder, early intervention and the availability of reliable preventive or remedial measures that are conscientiously implemented. Target groups of vulnerable or high-risk groups for appropriate detection and/or early intervention should be identified. The rationale for the potentially useful intervention should be explained.[1]

Various members of the task panel prepared papers and memoranda relevant to this charge. Portions of these documents, including

1

our own, were excerpted or summarized in the task panel report to the commission in February 1978 (Task Panel Reports 1978, pp. 1–130). Our contribution at the time and in the additional analyses that we have conducted since then were addressed mainly to the second and third paragraphs of the charge, which ask about the magnitude of problems of mental illness and their distribution in the population.

In trying to come to terms with these questions, we initially found ourselves in a position similar to that of the Michigan legislature when it was trying to draw up a code of law for legal commitment. The law-makers had to confront the problem that psychiatrists, legislators, and judges have been arguing for years over their various definitions of mental illness. There is little consensus within the mental health professions on this matter, much less between the mental health professions and the rest of society. Understandably, therefore,

> The Michigan Legislature was unable to sort out the conflicting opinions and omitted a definition of mental illness from its new code. Asked why, the chairman of the House Mental Health Committee . . . said bluntly, "We never could have passed the bill if we had to agree on that." (Mitchell 1975, p. 20)

Most data on the magnitude of problems of mental illness in the population and their distribution consist of records of patients admitted to mental hospitals and other treatment facilities. It has long been known, however, that such data are biased by a host of selective factors that determine who among those suffering from a particular type of psychiatric disorder actually receive treatment (cf. Dohrenwend and Dohrenwend 1969, pp. 5–7). As we show in Chapter 6, most of those who suffer from clinical psychiatric disorders have not been in treatment with members of the mental health professions and those who have come in to such treatment are frequently not typical of the far larger number of disturbed persons.

Yet once we abandon treatment status as the major criterion for determining who is a "case," we are confronted with the problem faced by the Michigan legislators, the absence of a clear consensus as to what should be included under such terms as "psychopathology," "psychiatric disorder," or "mental illness," or on how these phenomena should be measured (cf. Dohrenwend and Dohrenwend 1969, 1974b). Thus, although over 60 different investigators since the turn of the century have attempted to count not only treated "cases" but also untreated "cases" in over 80 communities in different parts of the world, the rates reported fluctuate wildly—not as a function of differences in the persons and places studied, but rather as a consequence of differences in the concepts and methods used to define disorder (Doh-renwend and Dohrenwend 1974b). For some communities, for exam-ple, reported rates of overall functional psychiatric disorders have ex-ceeded 50 percent of the populations studied. For other, similar communities, we have reports of rates of less than 1 percent, and vari-ations in between depending upon the breadth of the investigators' conceptions of psychiatric disorders and the thoroughness of the data collection procedures used (Dohrenwend and Dohrenwend 1974b, pp. 422–425). The situation is at least as chaotic in the smaller bodies of epidemiologic studies that have focused specifically on childhood dis-orders or on disorders of the aged, as we will show. The consequences of this methodological anarchy in the field of psychiatric epidemiol-ogy, as Kramer has strongly stated them, are that

> ... systematic statistics on the incidence and prevalence of mental dis-orders as a group, or of individual disorders within the group, do not exist for the U.S. or any other country. Major impediments to their develop-ment continue to be the absence of standard case-finding techniques that can be used in a uniform and consistent fashion in population surveys to detect persons with mental disorders, and reliable differential diagnostic techniques for assigning each case to a specific diagnostic category with a high degree of reliability (Kramer 1976, p. 188).

This state of affairs has not, however, inhibited speculation as to the true rates of psychiatric disorders in the population. Some of this spec-ulation has been put forth as official fact. It was possible to read in the *New York Times* (1975, p. 49B) just a few years ago, for example, that

> mental illness is "America's primary health problem," affecting at least 10 percent of the population according to the National Institute of Mental Health. Of the 20 million persons who suffer from some form of mental illness, one-seventh receive psychiatric care, the agency said. . . .

At about the same time, separate figures from the National Institute of Mental Health suggested that clinical depression alone affects 19–20 million people a year in this country (Bunney 1975, p. 5; WNET 1975).

It is difficult to know where the figures 10 percent or 20 million came from, but it seems likely that they were produced under the same kinds of pressures that are contained in the charge from the President's Com-mission on Mental Health. If sensible evaluations of existing policies are to be made and viable new policies created, it seems reasonable to want to know something about the scope of the problems to be dealt with. Figures have and will continue to be produced in response to such questions whether or not there is a warrant for them on the basis of adequate research. It is for this reason that we undertook analyses of the available evidence—not because we believed that the evidence is adequate, but because we wanted the basis for whatever figures are to be used to be explicit, even if it meant substituting hypotheses based on imperfect data for firm pronouncements whose basis is unknown. Such pronouncements have a way of perpetuating themselves, no matter how inaccurate they are. False hypotheses are more likely to be corrected by further research.

One deceptively reasonable way to approach the problem of lack of consensus as to how to define and measure psychiatric disorders in the general population would be to select for review and analysis only those studies that provided adequate evidence for the reliability and validity of their procedures for case identification and classification. Usually, however, there is no way to determine among, say, 20 or 30 epidemiologic studies that appear relevant to a particular question which are most reliable and valid for the simple reason that most studies do not supply evidence concerning the reliability and validity of their measures.

There are strong indications that this primitive state of methods in the field of psychiatric epidemiology is beginning to change. We say more about these new developments in the final chapter. Suffice it to say at this point that, by and large, the newer approaches have not provided the body of data on which we must rely to try to answer the questions posed by the charge from the President's Commission on Mental Health. Nor are they likely to for a number of years. Meanwhile, we must try to come up with best estimates on the basis of existing data that can serve both as guides for current policies and as hypotheses to be checked by more rigorous studies based on the newer methods now being developed. Given the problems just described, how did we proceed?

To answer the questions posed in the charge, we would like to know the rate of occurrence and distribution of mental health problems in the United States. More specifically, we would like to know the true prevalence of psychiatric disorders, that is, the rate of cases of such disorders in existence at a particular point in time or during a given interval of time such as a year, regardless of time of onset. We would also like to know the true incidence as indicated by the rate of new cases that arise within, say, the period of a year. To gain even a portion of such knowledge, we would have to learn the number of persons in the population of the United States who have problems of psychiatric disorder but who have never been treated by members of the mental health professions as well as those who have received and/or are receiving such treatment. How did we come to terms with the fact that such data do not exist?

Our approach was to focus on relatively small bodies of epidemiologic studies of communities in North America and Europe in which investigators attempted to detect cases of psychiatric disorders independent of treatment status. Accordingly, we excluded studies in which case counting was restricted to patients. This exclusion was extended to studies of the patients of general practitioners identified as having psychiatric problems because these studies appear to yield results that are unrepresentative of those obtained in community studies (Finlay-Jones and Burvill 1978).

Our procedure has been to search for trends in community studies, make extrapolations, and cross-check our inferences as much as possible by comparing findings from different methods. In the process, we have made some assumptions as to the meaningfulness of these data that should be made explicit. These assumptions center on the value of diagnoses in epidemiologic studies of true prevalence, the importance of the phenomenon being measured by psychiatric screening scales currently in use, and the value of a superior set of investigations conducted in Britain and involving systematic comparisons of different methods of assessing psychiatric disorder in children. Let us say a bit more about each of these assumptions.

Although the epidemiologic investigators whose studies we review and analyze in Chapters 3 and 4 differ to some extent in their methods of, and concepts and beliefs about, etiology, many of them present findings in terms of the same broad diagnostic distinctions. Thus many provide data on at least some of the following major types of functional psychiatric disorders: schizophrenia involving behaviors that come closest to the layperson's stereotype of what is insane or crazy; affective psychoses characterized by severe depression; neuroses whose hallmark is extreme anxiety and the panic, rituals, and phobias that can accompany it; and personality disorders that are too often manifested by persistent irresponsible and antisocial behavior and that include problems of addictions to alcohol and drugs. Moreover, there appears to be considerable agreement among the epidemiologic investigators as to the nature of these vividly contrasting symptom complexes or syndromes despite differences in where the investigators draw the boundaries among the different types and between all types of psychiatric disorders and "normality."

Our reason for believing that such a core of agreement exists about the nature of these disorders despite the lack of consensus as to their boundaries is that we found in previous analyses that there were consistent relationships from study to study between the various types of psychiatric disorders and important demographic factors such as sex, social class, and rural versus urban location (Dohrenwend and Dohrenwend 1969, 1974a, 1974b, 1976). These are the kinds of consistencies one would expect to find between, say, height and weight even when different investigators were using scales that were biased to register higher or lower than the true weights in a population and rulers that were biased to present people as taller or shorter than they are. Such consistencies we take as evidence that there is some essential truth and meaningfulness in the diagnostic data from these studies.

Although the majority of studies reported their results in terms of diagnostic categories, a minority of recent epidemiologic studies of true prevalence of psychiatric disorder have been based on screening scales designed to measure psychopathology on a single continuum from health to severe illness, without regard to type of illness. A major problem with these screening scales composed of objective test items is that they have proved to be only weakly and often only indirectly related to clinical psychiatric disorders of the kinds described earlier.[2] Nevertheless, we believe that the screening scales measure something important, something that we think can best be described in terms of Jerome Frank's concept of "demoralization" (Frank 1973). This phenomenon involves severe emotional and somatic distress that is likely to be experienced in association with a variety of predicaments, including, for example, chronic physical illness and stressful life events.[3] Our analyses of the prevalence and distribution of the syndrome of demoralization in the United States are presented in Chapter 5.

Finally, most of the epidemiologic data on the true prevalence of childhood psychiatric disorder in the United States is provided by studies in which teachers or, in fewer studies, parents have rated something that has come to be described as "clinical maladjustment." The two types of raters, teachers and parents, tend to see children in very different settings. The question arises, therefore, as to how to compare the results of the many studies that have used ratings by teachers to the few that have used ratings by parents, usually mothers. Fortunately, researchers in Britain have compared results obtained by the two types of raters on samples of children. Their analyses and results have provided us with strong clues as to how to analyze the U.S. data from the separate sets of studies based on ratings by teachers and ratings by parents. An account as to how we have developed and utilized these clues is contained in Chapter 2.

The state of affairs with regard to the data relevant to the questions contained in the charge from the president's commission is, then, far from perfect. However, these data proved to be far more substantial and intriguing than we would have believed possible before we undertook this task. The results of our analyses provide answers for today that must be tested and, when found wanting, replaced by better facts for tomorrow. But this will take some time.

Meanwhile, we present the results of our analyses not as firm conclusions but rather as the best hypotheses that we could formulate on the basis of the existing evidence. Because very few epidemiologic studies provide data over time, we have dealt mainly with prevalence rates rather than incidence rates. In the hypotheses we develop in the chapters that follow and summarize in the concluding chapter of this book, the term "prevalence" refers to a period somewhere between a point in time and about a year.

NOTES

1. President's Commission on Mental Health, 1977. Charge: Problem Definition Task Panel. Mimeographed.

2. Dohrenwend, B. P., Oksenberg, L., Shrout, P. E., Dohrenwend, B. S., and Cook, D. What psychiatric screening scales measure in the general population—Part I: Jerome Frank's concept of demoralization. Submitted for journal publication.

3. Dohrenwend, B. P., Shrout, P. E., Egri, G., and Mendelsohn, F. C. What psychiatric screening scales measure in the general population—Part II: The components of demoralization by contrast with other dimensions of psychopathology. Submitted for journal publication.

REFERENCES

Bunney, W. E. November 1975. As quoted in a report on the National Conference on Depressive Disorders in *The Nation's Health*, Washington, D.C.: American Public Health Association.

Dohrenwend, B. P., and Dohrenwend, B. S. 1969. *Social status and psychological disorder: a causal inquiry*. New York: Wiley.

———. 1974. Psychiatric disorders in urban settings. In S. Arieti (Ed.-in-chief) and G. Caplan (Ed.), *American Handbook of Psychiatry, Vol. 2: Child, and Adolescent Psychiatry, Sociocultural and Community Psychiatry*. New York: Basic Books.

———. 1974b. Social and cultural influences on psychopathology. *Annual Review of Psychology, 25*, 417–52.

———. 1976. Sex differences in psychiatric disorder. *American Journal of Sociology, 81*, 1447–54.

Finlay-Jones, R. A., and Burvill, P. W. 1978. Contrasting demographic patterns of minor psychiatric morbidity in general practice and the community. *Psychological Medicine, 8*, 455–66.

Frank, J. D. 1973. *Persuasion and healing,* revised edition. Baltimore: Johns Hopkins University Press.

Kramer, M. 1976. Issues in the development of statistical and epidemiological data for mental health services research. *Psychological Medicine, 6,* 185–215.

Mitchell, W. J. June 1, 1975. The insanity verdict: who is dangerous, who is sick? *New York Times News of the Week in Review. New York Times,* August 3, 1975.

Task Panel Reports Submitted to the President's Commission on Mental Health, Vol. 2, Superintendent of Documents, U.S. Government Printing Office, Stock No. 040-000-00391-6, 1978.

WNET Channel 13. March 31, 1975. *The thin edge: depression.*

2

FORMULATION OF HYPOTHESES ABOUT THE PREVALENCE, TREATMENT, AND PROGNOSTIC SIGNIFICANCE OF PSYCHIATRIC DISORDERS IN CHILDREN IN THE UNITED STATES

Madelyn Schwartz Gould
Robin Wunsch-Hitzig
Bruce P. Dohrenwend

Our task is to provide as accurate an estimate as possible of the prevalence of childhood psychiatric disorder in the United States. However, the state of knowledge in this field is such that the very definition of "psychiatric disorder" is even more at issue for children than for adults. An accepted nosology in child psychiatry has not yet been established.

CLASSIFICATION

Criticism has frequently been made of the low reliability of psychiatric diagnosis (Kramer 1965). This low reliability may be due to inadequacies of the nosology related to unclear criteria. However, recent years have witnessed considerable advances in the development of taxonomies of child behavior disorders.

One attempt at greater precision and comparability in childhood psychiatric disorders has been the multiaxial scheme developed by the World Health Organization (WHO). This multiaxial scheme, detailed in the ninth edition of the WHO *Classification of Diseases*, includes five axes: clinical psychiatric syndrome; specific delays in development; intellectual level; medical conditions; and abnormal psychosocial situations (Rutter 1977a). Early results on the evaluation of this multiaxial scheme (Rutter, Shaffer, and Shepherd 1975) indicate that psychiatrists found that this scheme made classification more uniform, was easy to apply, and corresponded closely to their usual clinical approach. A similar multiaxial system is being developed for the third edition of the *Diagnostic and Statistical Manual of Mental Disorders* of the American Psychiatric Association.

Another attempt to develop a standardized and reliable system of child behavior disorder has been the examination of symptom patterning by a variety of multivariate techniques (Achenback 1978/79). This type of empirical approach attempts to make explicit the judgment process involved in classification while minimizing assumptions regarding personality development and behavioral disorders (Millner 1975). Despite differences in methods and samples, a number of factor analytic studies have identified essentially similar factors (Achenbach 1978/79). These factors include (1) antisocial, delinquent, aggressive behavior; (2) withdrawn, anxious, inhibited behavior; and (3) mentation, developmental, and school problems. Because the goal of this research is to evolve a taxonomy that will make it possible to group children, not simply behavior items, recent research has used hierarchical clustering techniques to identify children who share similar behavior profiles (Langner, Gersten, and Eisenberg 1977; Achenbach 1978/79). It has been found that differences in profile types are significantly related to differences in the outcome of child guidance clinic contacts (Achenbach 1978/79).

Further research is necessary to validate both multiaxial diagnostic classifications and multivariate typologies. Rutter (1977a) suggested that useful diagnostic categories should differ in terms of family characteristics, biological features, age of onset, sex distribution, association with scholastic problems, etiology, response to treatment, and outcome. To produce such useful diagnostic categories will clearly require ambitious, well-coordinated, and sustained research efforts.

CLINICAL MALADJUSTMENT

Unfortunately, the majority of prevalence studies of childhood disorder have completely evaded the problem of classification by not clearly defining the clinical entities for which they have published rates. Rather, they seem to deal with the more global concepts of maladjustment and maladaptation.

Therefore, rather than reporting on the prevalence of "psychiatric disorder" as the totality of a group of clearly defined clinical entities, we report on the prevalence of a much broader range of clinical phenomena—usually described in this research as "clinical maladjustment." Despite its inclusiveness and lack of specificity, the concept of clinical maladjustment has often been used by public policy makers to assess mental health service needs (Glidewell and Swallow 1968).

Although the concept has limited value for deciding the types of services needed, it does provide a gross indication of the size of the problem, that is, the number of children in need of help.

Our estimate of the prevalence of clinical maladjustment is based on 25 U.S. studies conducted from 1928 to 1975. These studies are characterized by heterogeneity of both method and concept. In some studies questionnaires were administered to parents or teachers (Wickman 1928; Miller et al. 1971; Kellam et al. 1975); others employed highly detailed interviews (Langner et al. 1974). Still others used global approaches which allowed teachers to identify students as maladjusted according to the teachers' own criteria (Snyder 1934; Young-Masten 1938; MHRU 1964). Moreover, the concept of clinical maladjustment includes "problem children" (Hildreth 1929; Snyder 1934) and "emotionally disturbed" children (Bower 1958; MHRU 1964), as well as children described as "most seriously maladjusted" (Young-Masten 1938). Unfortunately, the conceptual differences or similarities in these descriptions are unclear.

The studies do, however, fall into two groups based on source of information: parent or teacher informant. The majority of the studies, 21, relied primarily on teachers as informants. They reported either point prevalence or prevalence for a brief period of a few months to a year. Most of these studies were reviewed by Glidewell and Swallow (1968) in *The Prevalence of Maladjustment in Elementary Schools: A Report Prepared for the Joint Commission on the Mental Health of Children.* The most recent U.S. studies, four in number, relied on parent rather than teacher reports. For comparative purposes, we also reviewed 10 British studies, four of which utilized multimethod, multistage procedures unparalleled in any U.S. prevalence study. The 35 studies reviewed are described in detail in the appendix following this chapter of the report.

There are inherent problems in comparing rates from individual studies using such heterogeneous methods and concepts. We have therefore grouped the results according to the broad type of assessment procedure used to see how much difference these major contrasts in method make. As Table 2.1 shows, there is surprisingly little difference in the average rates reported by investigators who relied on teacher ratings; on parent ratings; or on multimethod, multistage procedures. Equally surprising, moreover, is the fact that the U.S. studies and the British studies do not appear to differ in the average rates reported despite the fact that almost half the British studies used far more intensive case-finding and validating procedures than did the U.S. studies. What is the reason for this apparent consensus across methods and between countries?

TABLE 2.1

Rates of Childhood Maladjustment Reported in Studies Using Different Methods or Conducted in Different Countries[a]

	Both Sexes		Males		Females		Ratio of Males to Females[b]	
	Median	Range	Median	Range	Median	Range	Median	Range
Method								
Parent screening[c]	16.0% (9)	10.9–37.0	17.0% (5)	10.2–44.0	15.0% (5)	10.8–29.9		
Teacher screening[d]	10.8% (28)	6.6–22.0					2.1:1 (20)	1:1–5:1
Multimethod, multistage	16.5% (4)	6.8–25.4	15.7% (2)	13.0–18.3	18.5% (2)	10.8–26.2		
Country								
U.S.	11.8% (25)	6.9–30.0					2.3:1 (18)	1:1–5:1
British	13.2% (10)	6.3–37.0	18.3% (7)	10.2–44.0	11.5% (7)	8.1–29.9		
Total	11.9% (35)	6.3–37.0					2:1 (25)	1:1–5:1

[a]Number of studies on which median is based in parentheses.
[b]Actual percentages were not reported.
[c]Includes the results of the parent screening stage of the multimethod, multistage studies.
[d]Includes the results of the teacher screening stage of the multimethod, multistage studies.
Source: Compiled by the authors.

One possible explanation for the similarity in results based on teacher reports, on parent reports, and on the multimethod, multistage procedures is that they ar equivalent and, if applied to the same population, would all identify the same children. However, this is not the case. The issue has been examined in detail by both Rutter and his colleagues (Rutter and Graham 1966; Rutter, Tizard, and Whitmore 1970; Graham and Rutter 1973) and Glidewell and Swallow (1968). Rutter found that although parent and teacher screening instruments applied to the same population selected about the same proportion of children as being maladjusted, the overlap between the groups selected was only about 7 percent, that is, teachers and parents selected different children as maladjusted. Similar findings were reported by Mitchell and Shepherd (1966). Rutter explained the lack of overlap between parent and teacher selection in terms of differences between the child's behavior at home and at school. Glidewell and Swallow (1968) found that the level of agreement between parent and teacher was a function of social class—the higher the social class the greater the agreement between parent and teacher. Glidewell and Swallow, like Rutter, relied on a situation-specific explanation, suggesting that the difference between behavior at home and at school is greater in the lower classes.

Assuming that the parent and teacher informants identify different children as maladjusted, a better procedure might be one that utilizes the information from both informants. Only four studies, all British and all conducted by a single team of investigators (Rutter and Graham 1966; Rutter, Tizard, and Whitmore 1970; Rutter 1973b; Graham and Rutter 1973; Rutter et al. 1975), used both sources of information. Not only did Rutter and his colleagues use both parent and teacher informants, but in two studies they used the two informants in each of two stages of case identification. In the first stage both parents and teachers responded to self-administered questionnaires designed to identify children worthy of more intensive investigation. This second stage, an intensive investigation, designed to identify those children who were, in fact, disturbed, consisted of an interview with the parents, a report and questionnaire from the teacher, and a psychiatric interview with the child. The final identification of a disturbed child was based on the clinical judgment of a psychiatrist utilizing these three sources of information. It should be noted that questions have been raised as to the reliability and validity of clinical judgments (Oskamp 1965; Goldberg 1968). However, this multimethod, multistage procedure does give us some information about the effectiveness of parent sources of information as opposed to teacher sources. A diagram of the multimethod, multistage assessment approach used by Rutter and his colleagues is presented in Figure 2-1.

FIGURE 2.1.

Representation of the relationship of the teacher screen, parental screen, and intensive investigation in the multimethod-multistage procedure used by Rutter and his colleagues.

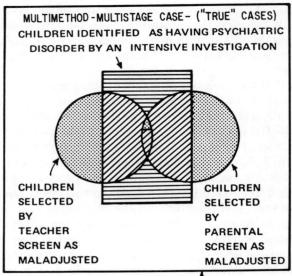

True Positives — Those children selected on screen as maladjusted and later identified as a 'case' by intensive investigation

False Positives — Those children selected on screen as maladjusted and later identified as a 'non-case' by intensive investigation

False Negatives — Those children not selected by screen as maladjusted, later identified as a 'case' by intensive investigation

MULTIMETHOD-MULTISTAGE CASE- ("TRUE" CASES) CHILDREN IDENTIFIED AS HAVING PSYCHIATRIC DISORDER BY AN INTENSIVE INVESTIGATION

CHILDREN SELECTED BY TEACHER SCREEN AS MALADJUSTED

CHILDREN SELECTED BY PARENTAL SCREEN AS MALADJUSTED

TOTAL POPULATION

Approximately to scale assuming an average "true" rate of about 16 percent for studies using multimethod - multistage procedures as shown in Table 1. However, it must be remembered that the proportion of false negatives fluctuates from study to study, i.e., seems to depend on location of study and age of population.

Source: Constructed by the authors.

14

Rutter found that about one-half of the children selected by the parent screen and about one-half of those selected by the teacher screen were finally diagnosed as having a psychiatric disorder. Of those selected by both screening procedures, 75 percent were finally diagnosed as having a psychiatric disorder. In terms of rates of true positives versus false positives, therefore, the parent and teacher screens were equally effective in that they selected equal numbers of disturbed children. However, a measure of effectiveness must take into account not only the number of children picked up on one or the other screen who are later identified as disturbed but also the number of children *not* picked up by either screen who are identified as disturbed, that is, the false negatives. Again, only the work of Rutter and his colleagues was directed at this issue. Although we have no information as to whether one informant screen results in more false negatives than the other, Rutter found that even a screen using both informants resulted in missed cases (Rutter 1970; Graham and Rutter 1973). As shown in Table 2.2, the correction factor for false negatives was, as expected, relatively large when only teachers did the screening. It also varied considerably, apparently as a function of the age of the children, when both teachers and parents screened for disturbed cases.

What implications do these methodological findings of Rutter and his colleagues have for our interpretation of the results of the 25 U.S. prevalence studies summarized in Table 2.1, specifically for the large majority of them based on teacher ratings only? If we make two assumptions, that the teacher ratings in the U.S. studies are similar to the teacher screening ratings used by Rutter and his colleagues and that the research settings in the United States are similar to those in London or the Isle of Wight, then the rate of maladjustment estimated from these U.S. studies would have to be adjusted in terms of the relationship among case-finding procedures shown in Figure 2.1. Specifically, the rate would have to be reduced by about one-half to account for the fact that only one-half of the children identified as disturbed by the teacher screen would be identified as "true" cases by an extensive examination. The resulting rate would then have to be approximately doubled to make up for the portion of the "true" cases that would have been screened by mothers but not by teachers—a piece of arithmetic that would leave us with approximately the same number, though not the same individuals, as screened by the teacher ratings in the first place. This coincidence may help to explain why the studies in Table 2.1 using teacher ratings, with a median rate of 10.8 percent, and studies using parent ratings, with a median rate of 16.0 percent, are as similar as they are to the studies using multimethod, multistage procedures, with a median rate of 16.5 percent.

TABLE 2.2

Correction Factors for False Negatives used by Rutter and Colleagues to Correct Estimates Based on Intensive Investigation of Cases Screened by Teachers and Parents or Teachers Alone

Source	Study Site	Age of Children	First Screening by	Sources of Data for Intensive Investigation	Correction Factor for False Negatives
Rutter, Tizard, and White-more (1970)	Isle of Wight	10–11	Teacher & parent	Teacher, parent, & child	1.25
Graham and Rutter (1973)	Isle of Wight	14–15	Teacher & parent	Teacher, parent, & child	2.73
Rutter et al. (1975)	Isle of Wight	10	Teacher	Parent	3.00
Rutter et al. (1975)	London	10	Teacher	Parent	3.20

Source: Compiled by the author.

There is a third corrective factor to be introduced. This factor requires that we increase the rate resulting from our previous two corrections to compensate for those "true" cases that would be missed by both the teacher and the parent screens. Unfortunately, as shown in Table 2.2, this factor appears to vary with such differences as the age of the children studied and the location of the research setting.

At this point, therefore, there is no way to provide a correction factor for false negatives on the basis of the work of Rutter and his colleagues. This problem serves as a reminder that we had best proceed cautiously in estimating the magnitude of clinical maladjustment among children in the United States on the basis of the results summarized in Table 2.1.

The majority of findings indicate that the rate of maladjustment for males exceeds the rate for females. In fact, this difference is found in 17 of the 18 U.S. and 22 of the total 25 studies that published rates according to sex. However, findings on sex differences have been shown to be markedly influenced by type of disorder. Whereas the rate of conduct disorders is greater for males than for females, the sex ratio is about equal for emotional disorders (Rutter 1977a).

Although we have quite consistent cumulative information on sex differences, the findings on age differences, social class, ethnic groups, geographic regions, and family factors are scarce. Some of these differences, however, are of considerable importance if confirmed by further research. In particular, although measures of disorders have probably not been directly comparable across ages, evidence suggests that the rate of disorder increases somewhat in adolescence (Rutter et al. 1976). In addition, using comparable methods to compare prevalence rates in different geographic regions, Rutter et al. (1975) found twice as much childhood disorder in an inner city as in a rural setting. Within such settings, moreover, there may be sharp differences according to ethnic background and social class. Langner and his colleagues (Langner, Gersten, and Eisenberg 1974) have data indicating that proportionately about twice as many black and Spanish-speaking children as non-Spanish-speaking white children in a section of Manhattan show severe psychiatric impairment. And Kellam and his colleagues (1975), studying a poor black urban community, found a rate that was the highest among the 35 prevalence studies. Within this poor black urban community Kellam, Ensminger, and Turner (1977) found, in addition, that the rates of disorder varied depending on family structure. Mother-alone families had the highest risk of maladjustment in the children, and mother-and-father families the lowest risk, whereas the risk entailed by mother-and-second-adult families varied depending on who was the second adult.

In conclusion, the studies by Rutter and his colleagues suggest that the rates based on single-informant studies—that is, parent only or teacher only—are probably conservative estimates of the true prevalence. Therefore, the prevalence of clinical maladjustment in the United States is probably no lower, on the average, than 11.8, the median rate based on all U.S. studies. However, we want to emphasize that the rates of maladjustment most probably vary across age, social class, ethnic group, and geographic region.

PSYCHOTIC DISORDERS

The majority of investigations of clinical maladjustment studied school populations. However, the prevalence literature on psychosis suggests that the more severely disturbed, psychotic children are probably not included in this type of sample. Of 35 psychotic 8–10 year olds identified by Lotter (1966), only one child was found in a school for normal children. Therefore, the rates of clinical maladjustment discussed above give no indication as to the prevalence of psychoses in childhood.

For a long time most investigators grouped psychoses of childhood together, usually under the term "schizophrenia of childhood" (Rutter 1977b). Recently, attempts have been made to differentiate "childhood schizophrenia" into a number of quite different syndromes (Rutter 1972; Eisenberg 1972; Kolvin 1974; Makita 1974). Except for autism, which has been called "the psychosis of childhood" (Rutter 1977b), there is very little information on the prevalence of childhood psychoses.

The only study of autism attempting complete enumeration of untreated as well as treated cases (Lotter 1966) found a rate of 4.5 per 10,000 in the County of Middlesex, England. Similar rates were found in two epidemiologic studies using treatment statistics only: 4.3 per 10,000 in Denmark (Brask 1970) and 4.8 per 10,000 in England (Wing and Hailey 1972). The only U.S. study (Treffert 1970) found the rate of autism to be 2.5 per 10,000. This rate is probably lower than the others due to the exclusion of cases on the basis of organicity and less thorough case-finding procedures (Wing et al. 1976). Studies providing information on sex differences found that males outnumbered females; Lotter (1966), Brask (1970), and Treffert (1970) found the sex ratios to be 2.6:1, 1.4:1, and 3.4:1, respectively.

Psychotic disorders are also rare in adolescence. Extrapolating from two community studies (Graham and Rutter 1973; Leslie 1974), Graham and Rutter (1977) suggested that the one-year prevalence of psychosis in midadolescence is probably less than 1 per 1,000. However, the majority of prevalence studies of psychoses in adolescence have been restricted to treated populations. Evans and Acton (1972) found only 1 percent of 239 new patients, aged 12–19 years, in an outpatient department to be psychotic. Steinberg (1977) found 5 percent of an outpatient population of 500 11–18 year olds had definite or probable psychotic conditions. Of these psychotic outpatients, Steinberg (1977) found that about 60 percent were diagnosed as schizophrenic. Even among hospitalized adolescents psychotic disorders are comparatively rare. Of inpatient adolescents, 14 percent and 9 percent were found to be psychotic by Warren (1965) and Framrose (1975), respectively. Bruggen, Byng-Hall, and Pitt-Aikens (1973) found 20 percent of the first 50 hospital admissions to be psychotic. Of these psychotic inpatients, Bruggen, Byng-Hall, and Pitt-Aikens (1973) found that 60 percent were diagnosed schizophrenic, a finding similar to Steinberg's (1977) outpatient population.

LEARNING DISABILITY, HYPERKINESIS, AND MINIMAL BRAIN DYSFUNCTION

In recent years there has been a spate of interest in learning disability, hyperkinesis, and minimal brain dysfunction. These disorders are frequently associated with behavioral and psychiatric problems and are therefore the concern of mental health professionals. However, these terms are often used synonymously (Walzer and Richmond 1973; Cantwell 1977) and semantic chaos so surrounds these disorders that research has provided no firm basis for understanding their prevalence. For a comprehensive review of the problems and findings in the research on these disorders, see Walzer and Richmond (1973), Minskoff (1973), Cantwell (1977), and Bosco and Robin (in press).

TREATMENT

The literature indicates that almost all psychotic children and adolescents are known to some treatment facility (Wing et al. 1976; Graham and Rutter 1977; Steinberg 1977). In contrast, findings on clinically maladjusted children suggest that the majority of these children were not receiving treatment. Of the 35 studies on clinical maladjustment, eight presented relevant information. The reported percentages of maladjusted children receiving treatment ranged from less than 1 percent to 49 percent in these eight studies. Table 2.3 summarizes the findings.

TABLE 2.3

Proportions of Clinically Maladjusted Children Receiving Treatment

Site of Study	Age	Source of Treatment	Percent Currently in Treatment	Percent Ever in Treatment
U.S.				
Snyder (1934)	Grades K–8	Special Services Dept.—includes psychiatrist, psychologist, visiting teachers, psychiatric social workers, attendance officers, and special police	8.6 (of all clinically maladjusted children) 19.7 (of the severely maladjusted children)	
Young-Masten (1938)	Grades K–8	Guidance clinic, probation officer, reform school	<1.0	
Langner et al. (1974)	6–18 yr	Mental health professional		30.0 (short-term treatment) 19.3 (long-term treatment, 6 mo +)

		Mental health professional	
Kellam (personal communication)	1st graders		<1.0
British			
Rutter, Tizald, and Whitmore (1970)	10–11 yr	"Any kind of treatment"—psychiatric treatment, probation officer, residential school, family doctor	20.0
Shepherd et al. (1971)	5–15 yr	Psychiatric treatment	<1.0
Graham and Rutter (1973)	14–15 yr	Child guidance clinic	10.0 (of all children with psychiatric disorder) 20.0 (of the moderately or severely disturbed)
Leslie (1974)	13–14 yr	Psychiatrist	5.0
		Psychiatrist	7.0
		Psychiatrist, general practitioner, school medical officer, pediatrician	49.0

Source: Compiled by the authors.

Two studies (Rutter, Tizard, and Whitmore 1970; Leslie 1974) suggest that the broader the definition of treatment the greater the percentage of children receiving help. Estimates of the percentage of children in treatment also vary depending on whether the investigators ever measure the percentage in treatment or currently in treatment. In addition, the data (Snyder 1934; Graham and Rutter 1973) suggest that the more serious the maladjustment, the more likely the child will be to receive treatment. Langner and his colleagues (1974), examining all children from well to severely impaired, also found that impairment level is related to the likelihood of treatment. Controlling for the child's level of impairment, other variables found to affect the likelihood of receiving treatment were the mother's level of education (Langner et al 1974), the mother's mental health, and the parents' tolerance of disturbed behavior (Mitchell and Shephard, 1966; Shepherd, Oppenheim, and Mitchell, 1971). The likelihood of treatment is greater the higher the mother's level of education, the poorer the mother's mental health, and the lower the tolerance of disturbed behavior.

CONTINUITY OF PSYCHIATRIC DISORDERS

To assess the mental health service needs of children, we should consider not only estimates of the prevalence of psychiatric disturbance but also the stability of disturbance over time. In estimating prevalence rates we have relied on cross-sectional studies, that is, studies conducted at one point in time. However, in order to differentiate transient disorders from more longlasting ones, a longitudinal design is the method of choice.

The majority of longitudinal studies examining the continuity and discontinuity of childhood disturbance have relied on the follow-up of children who have been referred to a treatment agency, few utilizing the follow-up of community samples. In addition, most studies involve short-term follow-up of two to six years, although some have followed their samples into adulthood. Findings are strikingly consistent among all studies.

Studies of both patient (Morris, Escoll, and Wexler 1956; Michael 1957; Masterson 1958; Annesley 1961; Warren 1965; Robins 1966; Masterson 1967) and community (Robins et al. 1971; Graham and Rutter 1973; Gersten et al. 1976; Robins and Ratcliff 1978/79) samples have found that the majority of antisocial children have a poor long-term, as well as short-term, prognosis. When antisocial behavior persists it is frequently accompanied by a wide range of other social and psychological handicaps such as marital disruption, poor work record, alcoholism, and drug addiction (Otterstrom 1946; Robins 1966; Robins et al. 1971; Robins and Ratcliff, in press). Although antisocial children do have poor prognoses, their outcomes are not uniformly unfortunate. Robins et al. (1971) found that even among the most highly antisocial children less than half were diagnosed as antisocial personality as adults and only 57 percent had any of the following diagnoses: antisocial personality, alcoholism, drug addiction. The stability of antisocial behavior seems to be related to family factors. For instance, Robins and Ratcliff (1978/79) found that when they were exposed to all of three family factors—being placed away from both parents, extreme poverty, and growing up in a family lacking parental figures of both sexes—89 percent of highly antisocial children were antisocial adults. Stability of symptoms has also been shown to vary as a function on the age of the child. Antisocial behavior appears to become stable only at or after 10 years of age (Gersten et al. 1976).

Childhood psychoses are very serious and persistent disorders. Follow-up studies (Eisenberg 1957; Annell 1963; Warren 1965; Eaton and Menolascino 1967; Rutter, Greenfield, and Lockyer 1967; Lockyer and Rutter 1969; Rutter 1970; Bender 1973) have shown that the vast majority of these children will not attain adequate adult adjustment. Most psychotic children spend much of their lives in institutions. The studies of autistic children (Creak 1963; Rutter et al. 1967; Rutter 1970; Kanner 1971; Lotter 1974) agree that about 60 percent of these children remain severely handicapped, unable to lead independent lives. Only about 15 percent make a good social adjustment, and even these children generally have continuing difficulties. An important prognostic factor is the child's IQ. Nearly all of those with an IQ below 50 end up in long-term institutional care. In contrast, autistic children with normal IQs have a much better prognosis. Few recover but about 40 percent improve sufficiently to hold a steady job (Rutter 1973a).

The prognosis for adolescent psychosis is also poor. Gosset et al. (1973), in their review of eight studies, found that between 12 and 61 percent of psychotic adolescent patients improved, with a median of 45 percent. The prognosis of psychosis varied with age of onset. The earlier the age of onset, particularly if prepubertal, the poorer was the prognosis.

In contrast to highly antisocial and psychotic children, most neurotic children become normal adults. Most follow-up studies, both long-term and short-term, have found that the prognosis for neurotic behavior appears to be rather positive in terms of later functioning. Unfortunately, most of these studies followed patient populations rather than representative samples of children. Robins' (1966) 30-year follow-up of 524 child psychiatric patients found that neurosis in adult life was no more common in the child patients than in a group of 100 controls. The other major long-term follow-up study (Michael 1957) found that children referred for withdrawal and associated emotional symptomatology were no more likely to be maladjusted than was a random sample of the population. Short-term investigations of clinic populations have also shown that neurotic children have the best outcome of all groups (Shirly, Baum, and Polsky 1940; Cunningham, Westerman, and Fischoff 1956; Annesley 1961; Warren 1965; Masterson 1958). However, a short-term investigation of a general population (Graham and Rutter 1973) found that although children with emotional problems fared significantly better than children with conduct disorders at a four-year follow-up, they had a much increased rate of psychiatric problems when compared to a control group. Despite this discrepancy in short-term findings, Rutter (1973) concurs with other investigators that the majority of neurotic children have a good long-term prognosis. Another short-term study of a general population (Gersten et al. 1976) agreed with the majority of findings that neurotic behavior in children is likely to dissipate or to improve. However, it was found that the prognostic significance of neurotic behavior depends on the age of the initial assessment of the disturbance. Gersten et al. (1976) found that up to middle adolescence neurotic disturbance is not stable and thus has little prognostic significance. However, this type of disturbance in middle adolescence showed greater continuity and thus its prognostic significance may increase.

In conclusion, two kinds of childhood disorders—highly antisocial behavior and psychosis—have a very poor prognosis for adult life. On the other hand, neurotic disorders of childhood have a very good long-term prognosis.

APPENDIX

TABLE 2A.1

U.S. Teacher Informant Studies

Study	Rate, Both Sexes (as given in article)	Rate, Males	Rate, Females	Rate, Both Sexes "Adjusted"	Rate, Social Class	Sample Size	Sample Description	Methodology	Comments
Wickman (1928)	7.0	—	—	—	—	874	Grades 1–6 Cleveland, Ohio "representative public school"	A scale of overall adjustment	
Hildrith (1929)	8.0	—	3 to 1	—	—	500	Grades 1–12 New York City 1 school	7 criteria to identify "problem pupils"	Also includes "a few" children chosen by psychologists or parents as exhibiting some problems
Yourman (1931)	11.0	—	—	—	"Some evidence of relationship . . ."	13,761	Grades K–8 New York City class and ethnic diversity	A scale of overall adjustment	
Snyder (1934)	6.9	—	5 to 1	—	"No evidence of relationship . . ."	11,998	Grades K–8 Jersey City, N. J. schools representative of city's population, ethnic diversity	Teachers identified pupils they considered to be "problems" and gave reasons for their choices.	2.6% considered serious behavior problems

25

Table 2A.1 continued

Study	Rate, Both Sexes (as given in article)	Rate, Males	Rate, Females	Rate, Both Sexes "Adjusted"	Rate, Social Class	Sample Size	Sample Description	Methodology	Comments
Young-Masten (1938)	10.0	3.6 to 1		—	—	11,150	Grades K–8 New Haven, Conn. all children in public elementary schools	Teachers identified pupils most seriously maladjusted and gave reasons for choice	
Rogers (1942)	12.0	3 to 1		—	5% affluent schools 18% depressed schools	1,524	Grades 1–2, 4–6 Columbus, Ohio 3 schools	Teachers rated children on modified HOW schedule, 9 other criteria including peer and observer ratings used	
Mangus (1949)	18.8	3 to 1		—	—	1,229	Grades 3 and 6 Miami County, Ohio Village and rural areas	Combined score from teacher rating, sociometric measure, and peer evaluation	Had author used 6 instead of 7 as cutoff point, he would have reported 11.1%
Ullman (1952)	8.0	12.6	3.2	7.9		810	9th graders from all white public schools in Prince George County, Maryland	Teacher asked to categorize each child according to 3 adjustment levels (each with accompanying description). The description next to "severe maladjustment"	High dropout rate, therefore ninth graders in sample represent those who stayed in school

26

Study	Rate (%)	Ratio		Relationship	N	Sample	Scale
Andrew and Lockwood (1954)	19.0	—	—	Some evidence of relationship	850	Grades K–12 Battle Creek, Michigan "representative sample of children in public schools"	reads "a child, who at his present rate, is likely sooner or later to have serious problems of adjustment and may need special help or care because of such problems." 11 item rating scale, each item having a 5-point scaled response set, 2% severely maladjusted
Glidewell (1959)	8.2	ca. 3 to 1	—	*	830	Grade 3 St. Louis, Missouri white only, class diversity	A 4-category scale of overall adjustment, *Sex and class interaction found (evidence of relationship true for males only)
Bower et al (1958)[a]	ca.10.0*	—	—	—	5,587	Grades 4–6 California class diversity	A 3-category scale of overall adjustment, *Estimated by Glidewell and Swallow (1968)
Gordon (1962)[a]	11.3	3 to 1	—	—	53,995	Grades K–6 Middlesex County, N.J. class and race diversity	A 5-point scale of overall adjustment
Gordon (1963)[a]	18.6	2 to 1	—	Depending on which method used, working class did or did not score more poorly than middle class	553	Grades K–6 Philadelphia, 1 school working class, race diversity	A 5-point scale of overall adjustment
	10.6	2 to 1	—	—	553	—	Bower-Lambert screening device,

Table 2A.1 continued

Study	Rate, Both Sexes (as given in article)	Rate, Males	Rate, Fe-males	Rate, Both Sexes "Adjusted"	Rate, Social Class	Sample Size	Sample Description	Methodology	Comments
								consisting of teacher, peer, and self-ratings	
Gordon (1963)[a]	11.8 / 20.0	2 to 1 / 2 to 1	—	—	Same as above Gordon 1963	445	Grades K–6 Jamesburg, N.J.	A 5-point scale of overall adjustment Bower–Lambert	
Lichten-stein (1963)	9.9	2 to 1	—	—	—	16,748	Grades K–6 Baltimore, Maryland	Identification of children according to 4 criteria of adjustment	Maladjustment meaning those children teachers thought special services
Woolf (1964)[a]	13.3	2.3 to 1		—	—	9,618	Grades K–8 Hunterdon County, N.J. mostly white	Gordon's 5-point scale of adjustment	
WHRU (New York State) (1964)	7.6	2.2 to 1		—	—	6,788	Grades 2–4 Onandaga County, N.Y. nonurban	Teachers identified those children they thought to be "emotionally disturbed." Investigators included children who were described as exhibiting similar behavior to children picked out by teachers	Excluded those children who had repeated a grade; 4.2% picked as emotionally disturbed by teachers. An additional 3.4% chosen by investigators
Springfield Services Dept.[a] N.J. (1965)	12.7	—	—	—	—	2,182	Grades K–8 Springfield. N.J. mostly white	Gordon's 5-point scale of adjustment	

| Stennett (1966) | 22.0 | 1 to 1 | — | — | 333 | Grades 4–6 Minnesota rural, white | Modified version of Bower–Lambert screening device consisting of ability ratings, achievement ratings, teacher rating scales, sociometric rating scales, and self-test. |

[a]Figures and descriptions abstracted from Glidewell and Swallow, 1968.
Source: Compiled by the authors.

TABLE 2A.2

U.S. Mother Informant Studies

Study	Rate, Both Sexes (as given in article) %	Rate, Males	Rate, Females	Rate, Both Sexes "Adjusted"	Rate, Social Class	Sample Size	Sample Description	Methodology	Comments
Miller et al (1971)	16.0	17.0	15.0	16.0	—	500	Grades 2–7 Louisville and Jefferson County, Kentucky	Mail questionnaire on 163 items of a behavior check list	Male and female rates calculated by authors.
Langner et al. (1974)	13.5	16.1	10.8	13.5	—	1,034	6–18 yr olds New York City racial, ethnic, and class diversity	Psychiatrist's ratings of structured questionnaires given to mothers. A 5-point impairment rating scale	Rate includes those who are markedly or severely impaired
Kellam et al. (1975)	27.7 30.0	—	—	—	—	863 1,391	Grade 1 (2 cohorts) All 1st graders in Woodlawn elementary schools. A Black, urban neighborhood in Chicago, Ill.	38-item symptom inventory	Children defined as "most symptomatic"

Source: Compiled by the authors.

TABLE 2A.3

British Teacher Information Studies

O.S.C.

Study	Rate, Both Sexes (as given in article) %	Rate, Males	Rate, Females	Rate, Both Sexes "Adjusted"	Rate, Social Class	Sample Size	Sample Description	Methodology	Comments
Douglas and Mulligan (1961)	8.0	—	—	—	—	4,109	Sample of children born 1st week in March 1946. 13 yr 2 mo. at time of study. Includes all birth of middle class and agricultural workers but only 1/4 of manual or working class. Great Britain	29 items, 22 of which were in form of rating scale	Although authors do not state "8.0% maladjusted," they do suggest that these are their findings. Also, that 4.5% severely maladjusted. Rates not adjusted for class bias
Pringle et. al. (1966)	13.4	15.6	8.1	11.85	Some evidence of relationship, more so for boys than for girls	9,817	Sample of singleton births born between 3rd and 9th of March 1958. 7 yr old at time of study. England	Bristol Social Adjustment Guide	Not clear whether school or clinical adjustment

31

TABLE 2A.3 continued

Study	Rate, Both Sexes (as given in article) %	Rate, Males	Rate, Females	Rate, Both Sexes "Adjusted"	Rate, Social Class	Sample Size	Sample Description	Methodology	Comments
Chazan and Jackson (1971)	19.5	19.1	9.8	14.4	Urban: middle, 6.4; working, 17.8; "deprived," 16.6; Rural: 11.5	726	Sample of children who entered school in Sept. 1968 and who were born between Sept. 1, 1963 and March 31, 1964. 5 years old at time of study. London and Wales, 26 urban and 11 rural schools	Schaefer's Classroom Behavior Inventory	Inventory used in U.S. but unpublished at time of this study. Rates for severely disturbed Total: .96 middle class: .71 working class:1.18 "deprived":1.13 rural: 0

Source: Compiled by the authors.

32

TABLE 2A.4

British Mother Informant Studies

Study	Rate, Both Sexes (as given in article) %	Rate, Males	Rate, Females	Rate, Both Sexes "Adjusted"	Rate, Social Class	Sample Size	Sample Description	Methodology	Comments
Ryle et al. (1965)	—	44.0	29.9	37.0	—	159	Ages 5–12 All children registered on the National Health Service List of 1st author, excluding families in social class 1 and 2	Psychiatric social workers ratings of loosely structured parental interview according to MacFarlane's 22 item, 5-point scale	Rates measure "psychological disorder as diagnosed by a general practitioner." Had the next cutoff point been used to define disorder, ratio for males would have been 18 and females 15
Shepherd et al. (1971)	10.8	10.2	11.5	10.9	Nonmanual: 17 Manual: 19	6,304	5–15 year olds Buckinghamshire, England representative of whole of southern England, though not necessarily of major urban areas such as London	22-item questionnaire	Had cutoff been 1 point higher or lower, total rate would have been 6.6 or 18.3, respectively
Leslie (1974)	17.2	20.8	13.6	17.2	No evidence of relationship,	1,198	13–14 year olds All attending local	Two-stage procedure:	Initial screening response rate only

Table 2A.4 continued

Study	Rate, Both Sexes (as given in article) %	Rate, Males	Rate, Fe- males	Rate, Both Sexes "Adjusted"	Rate, Social Class	Sample Size	Sample Description	Methodology	Comments
					however, numbers in social class I and II were small		authority secondary schools (excluding special and direct grant schools) Blackburn, England Industrial area	(1) screening based on parental questionnaire adapted from Shepherd. (2) more intensive investigation (consisting of parental interview and child's interview) of a sample of those children picked from the screening (i.e., stage 1) and a random sample of all those children whose parents returned the questionnaire	67.4%. Therefore, Leslie interpolated findings to reflect true prevalence rates (i.e., included findings from a sample of nonreturners). Rates not corrected for false negatives. Maladjustment defined as degree of disorder similar to those already attending child psychiatric clinic. Rates from stage 1 (screening of returners only): boys 25.5 girls 25.5 Rates from stage 2: severe: Total 4.4 boys 6.2 girls 2.6 moderate: Total 13.2 boys 14.6 girls 11.0

34

Not included as multimethod–multistage procedure since no correction for false negatives and no teachers reports

Source: Compiled by the authors.

TABLE 2A.5

Multimethod–Multistage Studies

Study	Rate, Both Sexes (as given in article)	Rate, Males	Rate, Females	Rate, Both Sexes "Adjusted"	Rate, Social Class	Sample Size	Sample Description	Methodology	Comments
Rutter et al. (1970)	6.3	—	—	—	No evidence from either screening or intensive study	2,193	10 and 11 yr olds born between Sept. 1, 1953 and Aug. 31, 1955 with the exclusion of those who attended private schools. Isle of Wight, England	Multistage: (1) screened teachers (26 behavioral descriptions) and parents (32 items, 18 of which identical to teacher questionnaire). (2) intensive study (parental interview, teacher evaluation, and psychiatric examination of child) of these children who appeared deviant on the teacher and/or parent screening questionnaire and of those children who were under care of any of the relevant services, all who had	2.06 severely disturbed 13.0 deviant from screen: 6.0 from parent screen; 7.1 from teacher screen. (About 7.0% identified from both screens, i.e., the amount of *overlap* of the two screens)

Study	N	Sample					Method	From screening
Rutter (1973) and (1975)	1,279 1,689	10 yr olds Isle of Wight and inner London borough. Excludes children whose parents are immigrants	Isle of Wight 12.0 London 25.4	13.0 18.3	10.8 26.2	11.9 22.3	come under the juvenile courts, known to a psychiatrist as of July, 1965, etc. Multistage: (1) screened teachers (adaptation of that used in 1966). (2) intensive study (parental interview) of those children who appeared deviant from screening *and* a randomly selected control group	IOW 10.6, boys 13.8, girls 7.1 London 19.1 boys 24.5, girls 13.2 Psychiatric disturbance *before* correcting for findings of control group: IOW 4, boys 6, girls 2.5 London 8, boys 12, girls 5 (Note: This is not same sample as 1970)
Graham and Rutter (1973)	2,303	14 and 15 year olds Isle of Wight	21.0	—	—	— (no evidence of relationship)	Multistage: (1) screened teachers and parents on comparable behavior questionnaires. (2) intensive study (parental interview, teacher interview, and psychiatric interview of child) of those children who appeared deviant from screening and other group who had been the	10.7 deviant from screen: 5.1 from parent screen; 6.6 from teacher screen (about 7.0% identified from both screens, i.e., the amount of *overlap* of the two screens); 7.7 identified as psychiatrically disturbed (2 males to every female) *before*

Table 2A.5 continued

Study	Rate, Both Sexes (as given in article)	Rate, Males	Rate, Fe- males	Rate, Both Sexes "Adjusted"	Rate, Social Class	Sample Size	Sample Description	Methodology	Comments
								juvenile court, been seen by a psychiatrist, etc. and a randomly chosen control group	correcting for findings of control group

Source: Compiled by the authors.

REFERENCES

Achenbach, T. M. 1974. *Developmental Psychopathology*. New York: Ronald Press.

————. 1978/79. The child behavior profile: an empirically based system for assessing children's behavioral problems and competencies. *International Journal of Mental Health*, 7.

Andrew, G., and Lockwood, H. 1954. Teachers' evaluations of the mental health status of their pupils. *Journal of Educational Research*, 47: 631–35.

Annell, A. L. 1963. The prognosis of psychotic syndromes in children. *Acta Psychiatrica Scandinavica, 39*, suppl. 172: 235–97.

Annesley, P. T. 1973. Psychiatric illness in adolescence: presentation and prognosis. *Journal of Mental Science*, 1961, *107*: 268–78.

Bender, L. The life course of children with schizophrenia. *American Journal of Psychiatry*, 130: 783–86.

Bosco, J., and Robin, S. Hyperkinesis: how common is it and how is it treated? (in press).

————. In press. In C. K. Whalen and B. Henker (Eds.), *Hyperactive Children: The Social Ecology of Identification and Treatment*. New York: Academic Press.

Bower, E. M. 1960. *Early Identification of Emotionally Handicapped Children in School*. Springfield, Ill.: C C Thomas.

Bruggen, P., Byng-Hall, J., and Pitt-Aikens, T. 1973. The reason for admission as a focus of work for an adolescent unit. *British Journal of Psychiatry*, 122: 319–29.

Cantwell, D. 1977. Hyperkinetic syndrome. In M. Rutter and L. Herson (Eds.), *Child Psychiatry: Modern Approaches*. Oxford: Blackwell Scientific Publications.

Chazan, M., and Jackson, S. 1971. Behavior problems in the infant school. *Journal of Child Psychology and Psychiatry*, 12: 191–210.

Creak, M. 1963. Childhood psychosis: a review of 100 cases. *British Journal of Psychiatry*, 109: 84–89.

Cunningham, J. M., Westerman, H. H., and Fischoff, J. 1956. A follow-up study of patients seen in a psychiatric clinic for children. *American Journal of Orthopsychiatry*, 26: 602–12.

Douglas, J. W. B., and Mulligan, D. G. 1961. Emotional adjustment and educational achievement: the preliminary results of a longitudinal study of a national sample of children. *Proceedings of the Royal Society of Medicine*, 54: 885–91.

Eaton, L., and Menolascino, F. J. 1967. Psychotic reactions of childhood: a follow-up study. *American Journal of Orthopsychiatry*, 37: 521–29.

Eisenberg, L. The course of childhood schizophrenia. *Archives of Neurology and Psychiatry*, 78: 69–83.

———. 1972. The classification of childhood psychosis reconsidered. *Journal of Autism and Childhood Schizophrenia*, 2: 338–42.

Evans, J., and Acton, W. P. 1972. A psychiatric service for the disturbed adolescent. *British Journal of Psychiatry*, 120: 429–32.

Framrose, R. 1975. The first seventy admissions to an adolescent unit in Edinburgh: general characteristics and treatment outcome. *British Journal of Psychiatry*, 126: 380–89.

Gersten, J. C., Langner, T. S., Eisenberg, J. G., Simcha-Fagan, O. and McCarthy, E. D. 1976. Stability and change in types of behavioral disturbance of children and adolescents. *Journal of Abnormal Child Psychology* 4:111–27.

Glidewell, J. C., and Swallow, C. S. 1968. *The Prevalence of Maladjustment in Elementary Schools: A Report Prepared for the Joint Commission on the Mental Health of Children.* (unpublished manuscript)

Glidewell, J. C., Glidea, M. C. L., Domke, H. R., and Kantor, M. B. 1959. Behavior symptoms in children and adjustment in public school. *Human Organization* 18: 123–30.

Goldberg, L. R. 1968. Simple models or simple processes? Some research on clinical judgments. *American Psychologist* 23: 483–96.

Gossett, J. T., Lewis, S. B., Lewis, J. M., and Phillips, V. A. 1973. Follow-up of adolescents treated in a psychiatric hospital. 1. A review of studies. *American Journal of Orthopsychiatry* 43: 602–10.

Graham, P., and Rutter, M. 1973. Psychiatric disorder in the young adolescent: a follow-up study. *Proceedings of the Royal Society of Medicine* 66: 1226–29.

———. 1977. Adolescent disorders. In M. Rutter and L. Hersov (Eds.), *Child Psychiatry: Modern Approaches.* Oxford: Blackwell Scientific Publications.

Hildreth, F. 1929. A survey of problem pupils. *Journal of Educational Research.* 18: 1–14.

Kanner, L. 1971. Follow-up study of eleven autistic children originally reported in 1943. *Journal of Autism and Child Schizophrenia* 1: 119–45.

Kellam, S., Ensminger, M., and Turner, R. J. 1977. Family structure and the mental health of children: concurrent and longitudinal community wide studies. *Archives of General Psychiatry*, 34: 1012–22.

Kellam, S., Branch, J., Agrawal, K., and Ensminger, M. 1975. *Mental hygiene and going to school.* Chicago: University of Chicago Press.

Kohlberg, L., La Crosse, J., and Ricks, D. 1972. The predictability of adult mental health from childhood behavior. In B. Wolman (Ed.), *Research in Child Psychopathology*. New York: McGraw-Hill.

Kolvin, I. 1974. Research into childhood psychoses: a cross-cultural comparison and commentary. *International Journal of Mental Health* 3: 194–212.

Kramer, M. 1965. Classification of mental disorders for epidemiological and medical care purposes: current status, problems, and needs. In M. M. Katz, J. O. Cole and W. Barton (Eds.), *The Role and Methodology of Classification in Psychiatry and Psychopathology* (DHEW, Public Health Service Publication No. 1584). Washington, D.C.: U.S. Government Printing Office.

Langner, T. S., Gersten, J. C., and Eisenberg, J. G. 1974. Approaches to measurement and definition in the epidemiology of behavior disorders: ethnic background and child behavior. *International Journal of Health Services*, 4: 483–501.

————. 1977. The epidemiology of mental disorder in children: implications for community psychiatry. In G. Serban (Ed.), *New Trends of Psychiatry in the Community*. Massachusetts: Ballinger.

Langner, T. S., Gersten, J., Green, E. L., Eisenberg, J. C., Herson, J. H., and McCarthy, E. 1974. Treatment of psychological disorders among urban children. *Journal of Consulting and Clinical Psychology*, 42: 178–9.

Leslie, S. A. 1965. Psychiatric disorder in the young adolescents of an industrial town. *British Journal of Psychiatry*, 1974 *(125):* 113–24.

Lockyer, L., and Rutter, M. 1969. A five to fifteen year follow-up study of infantile psychosis. 3. Psychological aspects. *British Journal of Psychiatry*, 115: 865–82.

Lotter, V. 1966. Epidemiology of autistic conditions in young children. *Social Psychiatry* 1: 124–37.

————. 1974. Social adjustment and placement of autistic children in Middlesex: a follow-up study. *Journal of Autism and Child Schizophrenia*, 4: 11–32.

Makita, K. 1974. What is this thing called childhood schizophrenia? *International Journal of Mental Health* 2: 179–93.

Mangus, A. R. 1949. *Mental Health of Rural Children in Ohio*. Wooster, Ohio: Ohio Agricultural Experiment Station, Research Bulletin No. 682.

Mangus, A. R., and Seeley, J. R. 1950. *Mental Health Needs in a Rural and Semirural Area of Ohio*. Ohio State Department of Public Welfare, Division of Mental Hygiene.

Masterson, J. F. 1958. Prognosis in adolescent disorders. *American Journal of Psychiatry*, 114, 1097–1103.

_____. 1967. The symptomatic adolescent five years later: he didn't grow out of it. *American Journal of Psychiatry, 123,* 1338–45.

Mental Health Research Unit, New York State Department of Mental Hygiene. 1964. Onandaga County School Studies, Interim Report No. 1. *Persistence of Emotional Disturbance Reported among Second and Fourth Grade Children.* Syracuse: New York State Department of Mental Hygiene.

Michael, C. M. January 1957. Relative incidence of criminal behavior in long term follow-up studies of shy children. *Dallas Medical Journal* 43: 22–26.

Michael, C. M., Morris, D. P., and Soroker, E. 1954. Follow-up studies of shy, withdrawn children. 1. Evaluation of later adjustment. *American Journal of Orthopsychiatry,* 24: 743–54.

_____. 1957. Follow-up studies of shy, withdrawn children. 2. Relative incidence of schizophrenia. *American Journal of Orthopsychiatry,* 27: 331–7.

Miller, L. C., Hampe, E., Barrett, C. L., and Noble, H. 1971. Children's deviant behavior within the general population. *Journal of Consulting and Clinical Psychology,* 37: 16–22.

Millner, E. S. 1975. Predictability of disturbed behavior, by age, over time in a cohort of urban children. Unpublished doctoral dissertation, Columbia University.

Minskoff, J. G. 1973. Differential approaches to prevalence estimates of learning disabilities. *Annals of the New York Academy of Sciences* 205: 139–45.

Mitchell, S., and Shepherd, M. 1966. A comparative study of children's behavior at home and school. *British Journal of Educational Psychology* 36: 248.

Morris, H. H., Escoll, P. J., and Wexler, R. 1956. Aggressive behavior disorders of childhood: a follow-up study. *American Journal of Psychiatry,* 112: 991–7.

Oskamp, S. 1965. Overconfidence in case-study judgments. *Journal of Consulting Psychology,* 29: 261–5.

Otterstrom, E. 1946. Delinquency and children from bad homes. *Acta Paediatrica,* 33: Suppl. 5.

Pringle, M. L. K., Butler, N. R., and Davie, R. 1966. *11,000 seven year olds.* London: Longman.

Quay, H. C. 1972. Patterns of aggression, withdrawal and immaturity. In H. C. Quay and J. S. Werry (Eds.), *Psychopathological Disorders of Childhood.* New York: Wiley.

Robins, L. N. 1966. *Deviant children grown up.* Baltimore: Williams and Wilkins.

Robins, L. N., and Ratcliff, K. S. 1978/79. Risk factors in the continuation of childhood antisocial behavior into adulthood. *International Journal of Mental Health* 7: 96–116.

Robins, L. N., Murphy, G. E., Woodruff, R. A., and King, L. S. 1971. The adult psychiatric status of black school boys. *Archives of General Psychiatry* 24: 338–45.

Rogers, C. R. 1942. Mental health findings in three elementary schools. *Educational Research Bulletin*, 21: 66, 69–79.

Rutter, M. 1970. Autistic children: infancy to adulthood. *Seminar in Psychiatry* 2: 435–50.

————. 1972 Childhood schizophrenia reconsidered. *Journal of Autism and Childhood Schizophrenia* 2: 315–37.

————. 1973a. Relationships between child and adult psychiatric disorders. In S. Chess and A. Thomas (Eds.), *Annual Progress in Child Psychiatry and Child Development*. New York: Brunner/Mazel.

————. 1973b. Why are London children so disturbed? *Proceedings of the Royal Society of Medicine* 66: 1221–5.

————. 1977a. Classification. In M. Rutter and L. Hersov (Eds.), *Child Psychiatry: Modern Approaches*. Oxford: Blackwell Scientific Publications.

————1977b. Infantile autism and other psychoses. In M. Rutter and L. Hersov (Eds.), *Child Psychiatry: Modern Approaches*. Oxford: Blackwell Scientific Publications.

Rutter, M., and Graham, P. 1966. Psychiatric disorder in 10–11 year old children. *Proceedings of the Royal Society of Medicine* 59: 382–7.

Rutter, M., Greenfeld, D., and Lockyer, L. 1967. A five to fifteen year follow-up study of infantile psychosis. 2. Social and behavior outcome. *British Journal of Psychiatry* 113: 1183–99.

Rutter, M., Tizard, J., and Whitmore, K. 1970. *Education, Health and Behavior*. London: Longman.

Rutter, M., Shaffer, D., and Shepherd, M. 1975. *A Multiaxial Classification of Child Psychiatric Disorders*. Geneva: World Health Organization.

Rutter, M., Cox, A., Tupling, C., Berger, M., and Yule, W. 1975. Attainment and adjustment in two geographical areas. 1. The prevalence of psychiatric disorder. *British Journal of Psychiatry* 126: 493–509.

Rutter, M., Graham, P., Chadwick, O., and Yule, W. 1976. Adolescent turmoil: fact or fiction. *Journal of Child Psychology and Psychiatry* 17: 35–36.

Ryle, A., Pond, D., and Hamilton, M. 1965. The prevalence and pattern of psychological disturbance in children of primary age. *Journal of Child Psychology and Psychiatry* 6: 101–13.

Shepherd, M., Oppenheim, B., and Mitchell, S. 1971. *Childhood Behavior and Mental Health*. London: University of London Press, Ltd.

Shirly, M., Baum, B., and Polsky, S. 1940. Outgrowing childhood's problems: a follow-up study of child guidance patients. *Smith College Studies in Social Work* 2: 31–60.

Snyder, L. M. 1934. The problem child in the Jersey City elementary schools. *Journal of Educational Sociology* 1: 343–52.

Steinberg, D. 1977. Psychotic disorders in adolescence. In M. Rutter and L. Hersov (Eds.), *Child Psychiatry: Modern Approaches*. Oxford: Blackwell Scientific Publications.

Stennett, R. G. 1966. Emotional handicap in the elementary years: phase or disease? *American Journal of Orthopsychiatry* 36: 444–9.

Treffert, D. A. 1970. Epidemiology of infantile autism. *Archives of General Psychiatry*, 22: 431–8.

Ullman, A. 1952. Identification of maladjusted school children. *Public Health Monograph* 7.

Walzer, S. W., and Richmond, J. B. 1973. The epidemiology of learning disorders. *Pediatric Clinics of North America* 20: 549–65.

Warren, W. 1965. A study of adolescent psychiatric in-patients and the outcome six or more years later. 1. Clinical histories and hospital findings. *Journal of Child Psychology and Psychiatry* 6: 1–17.

Wickman, E. K. 1928. *Children's Behavior and Teachers' Attitudes*. New York: Commonwealth Fund.

Wing, J. K., and Hailey, A. M. 1972. *Evaluating a Community Psychiatric Service: The Camberwell Register 1964–71*. London: Oxford University Press.

Wing, L., Yeates, S. R., Brierley, L. M., and Gould, J. 1976. The prevalence of early childhood autism: comparison of administrative and epidemiological studies. *Psychological Medicine* 6: 89–100.

Young-Masten, I. 1938. Behavior problems of elementary school children: a descriptive and comparative study. *Genetic Psychology Monographs* 20: 123–81.

Yourman, J. 1931. Children identified by their teachers as problems. *Journal of Educational Sociology* 5: 334–43.

3

FORMULATION OF HYPOTHESES ABOUT THE TRUE PREVALENCE OF FUNCTIONAL PSYCHIATRIC DISORDERS AMONG ADULTS IN THE UNITED STATES

Richard Neugebauer
Bruce P. Dohrenwend
Barbara Snell Dohrenwend

Epidemiologic studies designed to measure the true prevalence of functional psychiatric disorders in communities fall into two broad categories. The first are studies that base their case rates on clinical judgments by physicians, usually psychiatrists, of symptom data derived for the most part from face-to-face interviews with subjects. The second type, referred to here as screening scale studies, employ interviews that are designed to identify cases by means of objective scores on actuarily calibrated symptom scales rather than by means of clinical evaluations. Both sets of studies suffer from serious methodological problems. Nevertheless, they provide the best data available for formulating hypotheses about the rates of functional psychiatric disorders among adults in the United States.

We start with a review of the findings from clinical evaluation studies published in 1950 or later and influenced, therefore, by the changes in psychiatric nomenclatures that followed World War II (Dohrenwend and Dohrenwend 1974a, 1976). Because only eight of these investigations were conducted in the United States, we will discuss and assess their results in the context of 19 epidemiologic reports from other modern Western societies in Canada and Europe.

Although true prevalence studies of psychiatric disorders using clinical judgments constitute a reasonably discrete group of epidemiologic investigations, they exhibit considerable methodological heterogeneity. While some researchers utilized various random sampling methods to select their study subjects, others chose to interview the entire population of a geographically delimited area. In some studies symptom data were obtained through unstructured clinical interviews and in others by means of fully structured interviews employing fixed alternative response categories. In the latter type of study, the interviews were conducted sometimes by psychiatrists but more often by trained nonmedical personnel. When lay personnel administered the interview, the clinical assessment proper was conducted by the psychiatrist on the basis of a written protocol derived from the interview schedule. Although some studies restricted the information available to the psychiatrist regarding symptomatology to the data obtained in formal or unstructured interviews, other investigators emphasized ancillary record sources, the opinions of key community informants, and the observations of general practitioners serving the study population.

The procedure for identifying psychiatric cases and arriving at diagnoses for such cases also varied across studies. In some projects it was left to the implicit logic of "clinical judgment"; in others, subjected to rigorous explicit rules and criteria. A number of studies did not classify all diagnostic groups in a mutually exclusive fashion, whereas others used only mutually exclusive categories. Studies also differ dramatically as to the time interval under investigation. The measure of prevalence employed usually referred to the time of the interview, a few weeks, or the previous year. In a few studies, however, attempts were made to report lifetime prevalence.

It should be noted, too, that many investigators made an a priori decision to exclude from the study population persons in psychiatric or other institutions. As a consequence, these studies missed some cases of some types of psychiatric disorder such as schizophrenia and also of the acting-out types of personality disorder such as antisocial personality, alcoholism, and drug addiction. Furthermore, while some of the investigations reviewed here restricted their study populations to adults aged approximately 18–60, others included the elderly and, a few studies, children as well. In most cases, we have been able to recompute the rates reported in these latter studies so that they apply to adults below age 60 or 65.

SETTINGS AND PROCEDURES OF STUDIES

Eight U.S. Studies

A brief description of the eight studies conducted in the United States and published in 1950 or later will illustrate the heterogeneity of the methods employed. These studies, conducted between 1951 and 1972, reflect in their selection of settings and study populations something of the great diversity of U.S. society. Three studies (Dohrenwend, Egri, and Mendelsohn 1971; Srole et al. 1962; Pasamanick 1962; Pasamanick et al. 1959) were conducted in two major metropolitan areas on the eastern seaboard, New York City and Baltimore. At the other extreme are the epidemiologic works of Eaton and Weil (1955) and Shore and his colleagues (1973). The former researchers studied the mental health of the Hutterites, an Anabaptist religious sect of German origin, whose members live in small agricultural colonies scattered across the prairie states of North and South Dakota, Montana, and into Canada. The latter group assessed psychiatric morbidity among a Pacific Northwest coastal Indian tribe.

The three remaining U.S. studies examined sociocultural settings that are intermediate between these two extremes. Cole and his colleagues (Cole, Branch, and Orla 1957) evaluated mental health in a sample drawn from the predominantly Mormon Salt Lake City, Utah population. Trussell and his team (Trussell, Elinson, and Levin 1956) conducted their research in a rural New Jersey county, and Schwab and Warheit (1972) focused on Alachua County, Florida, a region experiencing a relatively rapid transition from a rural to an urban social structure.

The geographic and sociocultural variety in these U.S. investigations is matched by their methodological heterogeneity. Four studies, those by Dohrenwend and his colleagues, by Schwab and Warheit, by Cole and his colleagues, and by Srole and his colleagues, are based on probability samples varying in size from 257 (Dohrenwend, Egri, and Mendelsohn 1971) to 1660 (Srole et al. 1962) and drawn from a considerably larger general population, whereas Shore and his colleagues selected, from a total village population of only 200, a stratified random sample of 100 persons. In contrast, Eaton and Weil designated the entire Hutterite population, dispersed over 94 separate colonies, as their study population. However, only a small proportion of this group was evaluated directly by the project staff. Eaton and Weils' procedure was relatively unusual in studies done after World War II in that cases in the majority of the population were identified by means of interviews with colony leaders rather than interviews with the subjects themselves.

The studies done by Pasamanick and his colleagues and by Trussell and his colleagues are also special cases. Both drew random samples from populations stratified according to levels of disability. In the former study subjects were subsampled from a probability sample of 12,000 persons that had been drawn from the population of Baltimore. The physical morbidity of this probability sample had been established through a prior household interview and the subsample used for the psychiatric study was drawn in such a way that persons with severe physical disabilities were overrepresented. (Together with the rates derived from this investigation, Pasamanick reported rates based on institutionalized cases as well.) The subjects in the study by Trussell and his colleagues were also drawn in a similarly disproportionate fashion from a larger probability sample stratified according to disabilities.

These eight U.S. studies also adopted varying methods of obtaining symptom data. The designs of the Dohrenwend, Shore, and Trussell studies placed great emphasis on making direct contact, through personal interviews, between clinicians and study subjects. Trussell and his colleagues offered study subjects a complete, although apparently unstandardized, medical evaluation by a team of clinical specialists. Shore and his colleagues had two psychiatrists administer structured interviews to subjects, with subjects' responses, supplemented by data from community informants, rated subsequently by two senior psychiatrists not involved in the data collection procedures. The 15 psychiatrists in the Dohrenwend study utilized either a structured survey or a clinical interview and rated their respondents on the basis of the data collected in these interviews.

The research of Eaton and Weil, and Cole and his colleagues also employed direct contact between clinicians and study subjects, but these investigators did not extend this design to include all subjects who received mental health ratings, nor did they restrict their interview teams to trained psychiatrists. Although psychiatrists made the final diagnosis in all cases, in most cases the symptom data on which their clinical ratings were based were collected directly from subjects by nonmedical staff interviewers or were derived from secondary information provided by key community informants. In the Salt Lake City study, third year psychiatric residents and psychiatric social workers conducted largely unstructured personal interviews with one or two members of each participating household. Nonetheless, the rate reported in the study represented estimates of the total number of psychiatrically disturbed persons living either in the household or away in institutions.

In the three remaining studies, mental health ratings were made by clinicians on the basis of written records only. In the Pasamanick study the written records for the noninstitutionalized cases consisted of the subject's case record following a thorough medical screening. In the studies by Srole and his colleagues and by Schwab and Warheit, written protocols, derived from structured interviews administered by nonmedical personnel, were the basis for clinical ratings by psychiatrists. It may be noted, too, that all these studies, with the exception of the work by Cole and his colleagues, and by Pasamanick excluded institutionalized psychiatric patients in their estimates of rates of psychopathology.

Canadian and European Studies

The Canadian and European studies represent an equally diverse collection of sites and methods. Scandinavians have been particularly active in this type of research, accounting for eight of the 19 non-U.S. studies (Andersen 1975; Bjarnar, Reppesgaard, and Astrup 1975; Bremer 1951; Essen-Möller 1956; Fremming 1951; Fugelli 1975; Helgason 1964; Vaisanen 1975). Two true prevalence investigations were conducted in Central Europe, one in rural Austria (Strotzka et al. 1966); the other in two Polish towns (Piotrowski, Henisz, and Gnat 1966). A village in southern France was the subject of two different studies (Brunetti 1964; Brunetti 1973). The remaining European investigations are both British. One examined psychiatric morbidity in a northern Scottish parish (Primrose 1962). The other surveyed the mental health of residents in a new housing estate and an older residential district in Croydon, south London (Hare and Shaw 1965). Both Canadian investigations were conducted in comparatively rural settings on the Atlantic seaboard (Leighton et al. 1963; Llewellyn-Thomas 1960).

Although both U.S. and non-U.S. studies investigated mental health in urban and rural settings, the ratio of rural to urban sites is different in the non-U.S. studies, as is the extent of urbanization and ruralness of the sites. Of the non-U.S. studies, 12 were conducted in predominantly rural settings (Bjarnar, Reppesgaard, and Astrup 1975; Bremer 1951; Brunetti 1964; Brunetti 1973; Essen-Möller 1956; Fremming 1951; Fugelli 1975; Helgason 1964; Leighton et al. 1963; Llewellyn-Thomas 1960; Primrose 1962; Strotzka et al. 1966) and another three included both urban and rural locales (Andersen 1975; Piotrowski et al. 1966; Vaisanen 1975). In contrast, only four of the eight U.S. studies concerned rural populations.

A number of rural European sites are small, isolated communities cut off from the outside world to an extent unparalleled in U.S. studies (Andersen 1975; Bjarner, Reppesgaard, and Astrup 1975; Bremer 1951; Fugelli 1975) except for the Hutterite survey and possibly that of the West Coast Indians. On the other hand, only one non-U.S. urban study examined mental health in a major metropolitan area (Hare and Shaw 1965). The other projects have focused on small towns (Andersen 1975; Piotrowski et al. 1966; Vaisanen 1975).

Whereas the non-U.S. investigations employed the same range of data collection procedures as the eight U.S. studies, certain methods, rare in U.S. studies, were central to many non-U.S. investigations, and some approaches that dominate U.S. work were infrequently adopted in Europe. For example, five of the European and Canadian studies were essentially one-person operations in which a single investigator, usually the sole public health officer or general practitioner in a given area, conducted a survey of the mental health of the region's population (Andersen 1975; Bremer 1951; Fugelli 1975; Llewellyn-Thomas 1960; Primrose 1962). In these studies, information on symptoms was obtained through direct, usually unstructured interviews with a substantial proportion of the population in the catchment area. In some studies, these data on symptoms were supplemented by information from key community informants and medical records. In three other studies, a team of two to four psychiatrists conducted similarly designed population studies (Bjarnar, Reppesgaard, and Astrup 1975; Essen-Möller 1956; Vaisanen 1975). The Hutterite survey is the only U.S. project that placed comparable reliance on relatively unstructured interviews with a study population not selected by means of a random sampling procedure. However, in the Hutterite study, clinicians had direct contact with only a very small proportion of the population.

Among the four European urban studies (Andersen 1975; Hare and Shaw 1965; Piotrowski et al. 1966; Vaisanen 1975), which reported findings from six different urban sites, only two—the south London and the Polish projects—involved large teams of investigators. Like the U.S. studies, they utilized structured interviews, administered largely by nonmedical personnel. In the latter study, the interviews were analyzed later by several independent psychiatric raters.

In conclusion, we may say that both U.S. and non-U.S. true prevalence investigations selected widely varying study sites and adopted an array of data collection procedures and methods for arriving at clinical judgments. However, although three of the eight U.S. studies were done in major urban centers and seven utilized structured interviews for obtaining symptom data, only one non-U.S. study investigated mental health in a leading metropolitan area and only two employed a fully structured interview as the major method for obtaining clinical data.

GENERAL PROCEDURE FOR FORMULATING AN HYPOTHESIS ABOUT THE TRUE PREVALENCE OF FUNCTIONAL PSYCHIATRIC DISORDERS IN THE UNITED STATES

Given the extreme heterogeneity in data collection procedures and methods across studies, and the limited attempts to date to test the validity of these various methods of measuring psychopathology, it is not possible to restrict this analysis to a few clearly comparable, first-

TABLE 3.1

Types of Psychopathology for which Rates Are Available from True Prevalence Studies Based on Clinical Judgments and Published in or after 1950

Type of Psychopathology	Number of studies		
	U.S.	Non-U.S.	Total
All types of psychopathology	8	19	28
Psychoses	6	17	24
Schizophrenia	3	11	15
Affective	3	10	14
Neuroses*	5	18	24
Personality disorder	4	16	20

*In most studies that report rates for psychophysiological disorders this category is not mutually exclusive with neuroses. Consequently, we decided to omit specific discussion and estimation of rates for psychophysiological disorders since their inclusion would inflate unduly our estimates of overall rates of disorder based on estimates of the major subtypes.

Source: Compiled by the authors.

rate studies. Moreover, despite the fact that we have limited our analyses to studies using clinical judgments conducted in the United States, Canada, and Europe, and published in 1950 or later, the differences in concepts and methods used by different investigators have resulted in vastly different estimates of the rates of psychiatric disorders in the communities studied.

We will, nevertheless, attempt to formulate useful hypotheses about the true prevalence of psychiatric disorders among adults in the United States on the basis of the results of these studies. In doing so, we will rely on central tendencies across studies. We shall use the median rather than the mean because the number of studies is not large and some of them report unusually high or unusually low rates. This procedure of calculating central tendencies in rates across studies provides a set of estimates from the U.S. and non-U.S. investigations. The medians can be compared with each other and with evidence from research outside this group of epidemiologic studies of true prevalence to see if these estimates of central tendency provide a sensible basis for hypothesizing what the true average rates would be if a representative sample of U.S. communities were studied.

Nor are these central tendencies in rates all that we can extract from these studies. Enough of them provide data so that we can search for trends in sex differences and differences among social classes.

CENTRAL TENDENCIES IN RATES

Twenty-four reports presenting the results of 27 investigations conducted in North America and Europe appeared in or after 1950. Table 3.1 shows that, as emphasized earlier, the large majority of these studies were done outside the United States. Also evident are the consequences of the fact that each study did not provide data on all of the broad types of functional psychiatric disorders in which we are interested. Only half of the 27 studies, for example, provided data on affective psychosis.

Consider first the median rates shown in Table 3.2 for all studies in North America and Europe. The median overall rate is about 21 percent and the largest subtypes are neurosis with a median rate of about 9 percent and personality disorder with a median rate of about 5 percent. The median rate of psychosis, about 1.5 percent, is far lower and, within the psychoses, the median rate of schizophrenia is about twice the median rate of affective psychosis. Do the median rates for the eight U.S. studies depart from these estimates? Are there differences between the U.S. and the non-U.S. studies?

Table 3.2 shows that the medians for the total rates and for two types of disorder, psychoses and personality disorder, differ little between the U.S. and the non-U.S. studies. Within psychoses, only three of the U.S. studies reported rates for schizophrenia or for affective psychosis, too few for us to feel even minimal confidence in medians.

The one possible difference between U.S. and European results is in reported rates of neurosis. The median of about 15 percent for the six U.S. studies providing the relevant data seems higher than the median of about 8.5 percent for the 18 non-U.S. studies. Six U.S. studies is, however, too few to give us much confidence that the difference is real. Overall, the available evidence indicates more similarity than difference between the U.S. and non-U.S. studies.

Sex Differences

The ranges shown in Table 3.2 illustrate our earlier assertion that different concepts and methods have led to very different estimates of amounts of disorder in these studies. These methodological differ-

TABLE 3.2

Medians and Ranges of Rates for All Types of Psychopathology and for Major Subtypes

Type of Psychopathology by Geopolitical Area	Number of Studies	Median (%)	Range (%)
All types of psychology*			
N. America and Europe	27	20.85	0.55–69.00
U.S.	8	22.60	0.55–69.00
Non-U.S.	19	20.50	3.67–55.84
Psychoses			
N. America and Europe	24	1.56	0.00–8.30
U.S.	6	1.72	0.00–8.30
Non-U.S.	17	1.56	0.36–5.45
Schizophrenia			
N. America and Europe	14	0.59	0.00–2.68
U.S.	3	Too few studies	0.00–2.68
Non-U.S.	11	0.59	0.00–1.50
Affective			
N. America and Europe	13	0.29	0.00–1.91
U.S.	3	Too few studies	0.00–0.41
Non-U.S.	10	0.33	0.00–1.91
Neuroses			
N. America and Europe	24	9.38	0.28–53.51
U.S.	6	15.06	0.28–40.00
Non-U.S.	18	8.30	1.17–53.51
Personality disorder			
N. America and Europe	20	4.76	0.07–36.00
U.S.	4	7.02	0.07–36.00
Non-U.S.	16	4.76	0.88–14.86

*These rates include psychophysiological disorders for studies which employed mutually exclusive diagnostic categories.
Source.: Compiled by the authors.

ences make a comparison of absolute rates for males and for females directly across studies of little value. However, it is possible to compare the number of studies reporting higher rates for females with the number reporting higher rates for males. The picture that emerges from this type of approach is set out in Table 3.3, which shows that

TABLE 3.3

Comparison of Male and Female Rates of Different Types of Psychopathology

Type of Psychopathology by Geopolitical Area	Number of Studies in which Rate Is			Average Ratio Female–Male Where One Sex Tended to Have Higher Rate
	Higher for Males	Higher for Females	Equal	
Psychoses				
N. America and Europe	8	9	0	No trend
U.S.	2	1	0	No trend
Non-U.S.	6	8	0	No trend
Schizophrenia				
N. America and Europe	5	6	0	No trend
U.S.	1	0	0	No trend
Non-U.S.	4	6	0	No trend
Affective				
N. America and Europe	2	6	3	2.96[a]
U.S.	1	1	0	—[b]
Non-U.S.	1	5	3	2.97[c]
Neuroses				
N. America and Europe	0	18	0	2.86
U.S.	0	4	0	5.58
Non-U.S.	0	14	0	2.09
Personality disorder				
N. America and Europe	10	4	0	0.66
U.S.	1	1	0	0.89
Non-U.S.	9	3	0	0.61

[a]This ratio is misleadingly high because in the two studies in which the rate for males was higher than the rate for females, the latter rate was 0, and consequently no value could be assigned to the ratio.

[b]Ratios could not be calculated for these studies from the information available.

[c]This ratio is misleadingly high because a study reporting a zero rate for females could not be included in these calculations.

Source: Compiled by the authors.

there is no clear pattern of sex differences for the psychoses in general or for schizophrenia in particular. There is, however, a trend for affective psychoses to be higher for women. Moreover, for neurosis and personality disorder, the consistency of the sex differences is striking: There is a clear pattern across studies whereby higher rates of neuroses are reported for women and higher rates of personality disorder for men. Moreover, the pattern for the neuroses appears to hold in the U.S. as well as the non-U.S. studies. Unfortunately, only two U.S. studies provided data on personality disorder according to sex.

Note that not only are there consistent sex differences for neurosis and personality disorder but also that the magnitude of these differences appears to be large. In the case of the neuroses, for example, females appear on the average to have greater than twice the rate of males. As noted earlier, the antisocial and addictive types of personality disorder, which are far more prevalent in males than in females, are likely to be undercounted in cross-sectional studies such as these because many people given these diagnoses spend part of their lives in prison or other institutions. For this reason the ratios of the sex differences for personality disorders may be much higher than those shown in Table 3.3.

Social Class

Of the investigations conducted in North America and Europe and published in or after 1950, 21 reported rates of psychiatric disorders by social class. The distribution of these studies according to geopolitical site and the relative magnitude of the rate reported for the lowest class compared to other social classes is summarized in Table 3.4 Clearly the great majority of these studies found a relatively high frequency of psychopathology in the lowest stratum.

TABLE 3.4

Number of True Prevalence Studies Reporting Highest Rates of All Types of Psychopathology in the Lowest Social Class and in Other than the Lowest Social Class

Study Site	Number of Studies in which Rate Is Highest for	
	Lowest Class	Other than Lowest Class
N. America and Europe	15	6
U.S.	5	1
Non-U.S.	10	5

Source: Compiled by the authors.

TABLE 3.5

Comparison of Rates Reported for All Types of Psychopathology in Highest and Lowest Social Classes

Study Site	Number of Studies in which the Rate Is Higher for		Average Ratio Low–High Class
	Lowest Class	Highest Class	
N. America and Europe	17	3	2.59
U.S.	5	1	2.37
Non-U.S.	13	2	2.73

Source: Compiled by the authors.

In some of the investigations that reported the highest rate in the lowest class, the middle class showed the lowest rate and the upper class occupied an intermediate place. However, in order to have a standard basis for calculating the ratio between rates in different classes our comparisons will be made between rates of disorder reported in the lowest class and rates reported in the highest class, irrespective of whether the latter showed the lowest rate of all classes analyzed.

Table 3.5 presents the number of studies reporting the highest rate of all types of psychopathology for the lowest social class as compared with the number reporting the maximum rate for the highest class. As expected, the lowest social stratum is almost always reported to have a higher rate of disorder than the highest class. In U.S. studies alone, only one out of six studies failed to show this finding. In the 15 non-U.S. studies providing the relevant data, this relationship appeared in all but two. Across all studies, psychopathology in general was found to be at least two and a half times more prevalent in the lowest class than in the highest class.

Rates of psychopathology in general are not the best information for determining the distribution of the social and personal burdens associated with mental illness because they include disorders that vary widely in severity and type. For illumination of this issue we will consider the social class distribution of specific diagnostic subtypes.

Table 3.6 summarizes the findings from the eight North American and European studies that reported separate rates by class for the psychoses. Of eight studies, six reported higher rates in the lowest class, one reported approximately the same rates in both the highest and

TABLE 3.6

Comparison of Rates for Psychoses in
Highest and Lowest Social Classes

Study Site	Number of Studies in which Rate Is Higher for		Approximately Equal in Two Classes	Average Ratio Low–High Class
	Lowest Class	Highest Class		
N. America and Europe	6	1	1	2.06
U.S.	2	1	1	2.58
Non-U.S.	4	0	0	1.36

Source: Compiled by the authors.

lowest classes, and the final study found psychoses more frequent in the highest class. Although the two studies failing to find an excess of psychoses in the lowest class are both of U.S. origin, it is not possible to interpret this finding with any confidence, given the small number of studies involved. These study findings indicate that the severest disorders are also, on an average, twice as common in the lowest class than in the highest class. We should note that this class difference is probably due to an excess of schizophrenia in the lowest class because affective psychoses have rarely been found to occur at a relatively high rate in this class (cf. Dohrenwend and Dohrenwend 1974a, p. 440).

TABLE 3.7

Comparison of Rates for the Neuroses in
Highest and Lowest Social Classes

Study Site	Number of Studies in which the Rate Is Higher for		Average Ratio Low–High Class where One Class Tended to Have Higher Rate
	Lowest class	Highest Class	
N. America and Europe	5	4	No trend
U.S.	3	1	1.34
Non-U.S.	2	3	No trend

Source: Compiled by the authors.

TABLE 3.8

Comparison of Rates of Personality Disorders in Highest and Lowest Social Classes

| | Number of Studies in which the Rate Is Higher for | | Average Ratio Low–High Class |
Study Site	Lowest Class	Highest Class	
N. America and Europe	5	1	1.77
U.S.	2	0	3.31*
Non-U.S.	3	1	1.39

*This figure represents the ratio from only one of two studies. The other study reported no personality disorder in the highest class, thereby making the calculation of a ratio between the rate in the lowest and the highest class mathematically meaningless.

Source: Compiled by the authors.

Neuroses are close to the other end of the spectrum of severity from the psychoses. Nine studies altogether, with four in the United States, reported rates for the neuroses by class. Their findings are summarized in Table 3.7.

No clear pattern emerges from this table, of either a direct or inverse relationship between class and neuroses. Although the U.S. studies considered alone suggest a possible excess of neuroses in the lowest class, there are too few studies to sustain any conclusions in this regard, particularly in light of the lack of a clear association in the non-U.S. studies.

Personality disorders represent a sizable burden on the community because alcoholism, drug addiction, and antisocial personality are included under this rubric. Table 3.8 indicates dramatically the general tendency for personality disorders to be more frequent in the lowest class than in the highest class. Of the six studies reporting rates for personality disorder by social class, only one showed a higher rate in the highest class. Both U.S. studies reported a sizable predominance of personality disorder in the lowest class. The magnitude of the relative difference in rates between the two classes in the United States is not fully reflected in the average ratio column. In one U.S. study, the rate in the lowest class was 6.7 per 100 whereas the rate in the highest class was 0. As a consequence, no ratio could be computed for this particular study.

MEANING OF THE MEDIAN RATES

When problems of measurement are as great and as unresolved as they are in these epidemiologic studies of true prevalence, it is mandatory to be cautious about interpreting the results. The nature of these problems of measurement are such, however, that we are more skeptical about some results than others. We place considerably more confidence in the consistent relationships found between sex and various types of disorders than we do in the median rates of various types of disorders as estimates of the true rates in the United States or anywhere else.

An analogy may help to explain why we make this judgment. Consider what might happen if a group of researchers used rulers and scales that were grossly imperfect in different ways. Some rulers measured people as too tall; others as too short. Some scales weighed light; others heavy. Unless we had precise knowledge of the nature of these measurement biases it would make little sense to compare different communities investigated by differently biased measures because the subject differences and measurement differences would be confounded. Nevertheless, it is likely that the true relationship between height and weight is so strong that a positive correlation would survive the biased measuring instruments.

As is evident in the preceding analyses of the epidemiologic studies, we have not attempted to compare rates reported by different investigators using different measures in the various communities studied. We have, however, presented the average of these rates in the form of medians for consideration as useful estimates of the true rates. In doing so, we have made implicit assumptions as to the nature of the measurement biases involved in these studies and also as to the representativeness of the communities studied. Of the two sets of assumptions, we think that the latter is the less problematic. Although eight U.S. communities are certainly not a random sample of U.S. communities, they are very diverse. Moreover, the median rate of functional disorder and the median rates of the subtypes of disorder for these communities are consistent with the 19 non-U.S. communities that, although not a random sample of Canadian and European communities, are also diverse. The fact that the medians for the quite different samples of U.S. and non-U.S. communities are so similar suggests that if a truly random sample of 27 U.S. communities had been studied by the same 24 investigators whose results are summarized in Table 3.2, the median rates would not be very different.

However, what confidence can we have in the median rates of functional psychiatric disorders calculated from the separate rates reported in these studies, given the measurement contrasts involved? Can we assume, as has been implied, that the measurement biases are unsystematic and cancel each other out, leaving us with quite an accurate estimate of the average true rate? We most assuredly cannot make such an assumption. The ranges in rates shown in Table 3.2 indicate that there were, to be sure, studies that used broad and studies that used narrow conceptions of disorders in defining a case. Nevertheless, in deciding to consider only studies published after 1950, we opted for investigations using relatively broad definitions of a case because it was at about this time that expanded nomenclatures came into being. As shown in an earlier analysis of investigations all over the world that had used direct interviews with all subjects in the communities studied, this shift to expanded conceptions of disorder was accompanied by an increase in the median for all types of disorder combined from slightly under 4 percent to close to 20 percent (Dohrenwend and Dohrenwend 1974a). Moreover, the expansion of the definition of cases of disorder with corresponding increases in the rates reported tended to continue in the 1960s and 1970s (Dohrenwend and Dohrenwend 1976). Who is to say where truth lies in these historic swings of the pendulum between broader and narrower definitions?

Suffice it to say, our medians are probably biased largely in one direction, toward broader definitions and higher rates, by virtue of the decision we made to focus on studies published in 1950 or later. Nor would it help matters to include the studies published prior to 1950. Worldwide, only six of the 16 earlier studies involved direct interviews with study subjects; the remaining 10 relied wholly on either key informants or official records, a procedure that tends to reduce the number of cases counted due to inadequate coverage. The result is that not only would we be able to add very few studies, but the rates for those studies would tend to be discontinuously low in relation to the later studies. Let us therefore return to the medians presented in Table 3.2 with the possibility in mind that they are biased upward. In examining the possibility, we will go outside the evidence from the epidemiologic studies of true prevalence and consider evidence from other investigations of the major types of functional psychiatric disorders.

Schizophrenia

Table 3.2 shows that 0.59 was the median of the prevalence rates of schizophrenia reported in the 14 North American and European studies published in 1950 or later from which we could extract the information. There were too few U.S. studies for us to calculate a median rate for the U.S. alone. Does this figure of 0.59 provide a reasonable hypothesis as to the average prevalence of schizophrenia in U.S. communities?

The most complete record of treated cases of psychiatric disorder anywhere in the United States is in Monroe County, New York.[1] Here the Department of Psychiatry of the University of Rochester has maintained a psychiatric register that includes patients in treatment with private psychiatrists as well as patients reported by all other outpatient and inpatient facilities that provide psychiatric services to residents of the county (Babigian 1975). Moreover, these data are kept in such a form that unduplicated counts of treated disorders with various diagnoses can be made. The period prevalence for adults below age 65 based on such counts was 0.73 percent for the year 1970 (Babigian 1975). This figure is slightly higher than the 0.36 percent prevalence of treated schizophrenia for the period of six months reported by Hollingshead and Redlich (1958) in their research in New Haven, which also included coverage of private psychiatrists.

These figures for treated prevalence and our median true prevalence rates are below those for the lifetime true prevalence of schizophrenia reported in several Scandinavian studies published before 1950 as well as later (cf. Dohrenwend and Dohrenwend 1969; Dunham 1965; Yolles and Kramer 1969). Rather, the lifetime rates for the true prevalence of schizophrenia reported in these studies seem in line with Kringlen's conclusion that "the morbidity risk for schizoprenia in Scandinavia is observed to be around .9 per cent with a range of .65–2.85 per cent" (1976, p. 432). Moreover, the treated prevalence rates and our median true prevalence rate are below the period prevalence rates of 1.7 and 2.2 percent in two groups of relatives of control adoptees that Kety and his colleagues studied in their research on genetic factors in schizophrenia in Denmark (Kety et al. 1976, pp. 418–19). Like the lifetime true prevalence rates discussed above, these findings are not limited to subjects in psychiatric treatment. However, Kety and his colleagues used a U.S. definition of schizophrenia that is broader than the traditional European definition. The European definition emphasizes "chronicity and severity of cardinal features" (Kety et al. 1976). By contrast, the U.S. definition included, in addition to this traditional type of severe chronic schizophrenia, two additional syndromes called "latent or borderline schizophrenia" and "acute schizophrenic reaction."

These rates from Kety and his colleagues are not dissimilar to the one of 2.68 percent found but not published up to now, as a composite from two samples from the Washington Heights section of New York City. The subjects in this study were interviewed by psychiatrists (e.g.,

Dohrenwend, Egri, and Mendelsohn 1971). The Washington Heights study comprised of 257 adults drawn from the general population did not include schizophrenics who were hospitalized at the time of study. To do so would in all likelihood lead to an upward adjustment in the rate. In the context of such figures, the median of 0.59 percent from the true prevalence studies that we reviewed appears to be very conservative. Whether a figure like 0.59 percent represents a good hypothesis about what the average true prevalence of schizophrenia would be if we studied a representative sample of U.S. communities would depend, we think, on whether one used a definition including both borderline and acute schizophrenic reaction along with severe chronic schizophrenia.

Probably the best indication of the diagnostic conventions likely to be followed in most future research in the United States can be found in the Research Diagnostic Criteria (RDC),[2] developed to parallel the new APA Diagnostic and Statistical Manual (DSM III) which will be published during the next few years. Thus far, only one epidemiologic study has been conducted using RDC criteria (Weissman, Myers, and Harding 1978a,b). For the present, this study in New Haven, Connecticut must be considered one of a kind, first, because it is the only one to use RDC, and second, because the diagnoses were made by two interviewers with predoctoral levels of education. Although both had clinical experience, they differed in background from the diagnosticians in the other studies considered here. For both reasons, we did not include the New Haven study among the other true prevalence studies reviewed. This gives us the opportunity now to investigate the results of this study using RDC criteria with regard to our problem of whether the medians for schizophrenia and other disorders in the larger array of true prevalence studies are overestimates.

The point prevalence rate of RDC schizophrenia found in the sample of 399 New Haven adults age 65 and younger was 0.5 percent. An additional 0.25 percent received the diagnosis of "borderline features." And still another 0.25 percent were diagnosed "unspecified functional psychosis," a category that does not include affective psychoses. If we allow for the fact that this study did not include institutionalized schizophrenics, it does not seem unreasonable to think that this point prevalence rate of clear cut RDC schizophrenia in New Haven would have to be adjusted upward to at least 0.6 percent.

Strauss and Gift (1977) argued that the existing state of knowledge is such that we should avoid premature closure on questions as to whether narrower or broader definitions of schizophrenia will ultimately prove more useful. On the basis of this type of argument and the existing evidence, then, we think that a reasonable hypothesis about the prevalence of schizophrenia in the United States for a period of a few weeks to a year is that it will be on the average somewhere between 0.6 percent and 3.0 percent, depending on how many of the now seriously considered varieties or subtypes of schizophrenia are included in the definition. The reasoning is that rates from the true prevalence studies in Canada and Europe hover around 0.6 percent, as does the New Haven rate for RDC diagnoses. We assume that these figures, secured with relatively narrow definitions of schizophrenia, tend to be underestimates, if only because most do not include cases in institutions at the time of the study. On the other hand, even with the addition of such cases, the figure of 0.6 percent will be nowhere near the figures of 2–3 percent reported in studies in Copenhagen by Kety and his colleagues and in Washington Heights by Dohrenwend and his colleagues. With such broader definitions, and with inclusion of institutionalized cases, we think that it is not unreasonable to hypothesize that the average rate may prove nearer to 3 percent.

Affective Psychosis

The median rate for affective psychosis is 0.29 percent in the North American and European communities shown in Table 3.2. We have no better hypothesis than this estimate, which we should place at about 0.3 percent to account for institutionalized cases, as to what the true period prevalence for such disorder would be on the average in U.S. communities. Thinking about how to measure and classify the affective disorders is undergoing great change, and it is not clear as to how to get from the types of severe depression counted by the studies summarized in Table 3.2 to the classifications in current drafts of DSM III or Research Diagnostic Criteria. This difficulty is underlined by the fact that the prevalence rate from the New Haven study for RDC "major depression" is 4.0 percent (Weissman and Myers and Harding 1978a), well beyond any rate reported for affective psychosis in North American or European studies.[3]

Neurosis

Table 3.2 shows a difference in the U.S. and non-U.S. medians for neurosis. The median for the non-U.S. studies is 8.3 percent by contrast to 15.6 percent for the U.S. studies. One possible reason for this difference is that rates of neurosis tend to be higher in urban than rural settings (Dohrenwend and Dohrenwend 1974a) and a larger portion of the non-U.S. studies, as noted earlier, were in rural settings. If this is the reason for the difference, the U.S. median is more suitable for our purposes because the large majority of U.S. residents live in urban settings. Another possible reason, however, is that the European investigators use more restrictive criteria than the U.S. investigators in diagnosing neurosis.

Let us consider again the RDC diagnosis from New Haven as a possible source of clues. RDC does not include a diagnosis of neurosis. Instead, it lists several diagnoses that are probably close in content to what would conventionally be considered neurosis. These include "minor depression," "generalized anxiety," "phobic disorder," and "panic disorder," all of which were given to one or more of the New Haven respondents—7.5 percent of them all told. This figure is clearly nearer the Table 3.2 median of 8.3 percent for non-U.S. studies than for U.S. studies. However, we do not know what portion of the 4 percent of New Haven subjects diagnosed "major depression" would be in the neurotic rather than the psychotic category by DSM I or DSM II rather than DSM III classification procedures. Thus, it seems unreasonable at this point to choose between either of the medians in Table 3.2 as the better basis for our hypothesis as to what the rates of neurosis would be in the average U.S. community. We will suggest that they would be between the medians for the U.S. and non-U.S. studies, that is, between about 8 percent and 15 percent.

Personality Disorder

The median rate of personality disorder shown in Table 3.2 is close to 5 percent for all 20 of the North American and European studies that provided relevant data. For the four U.S. studies, the median of about 7 percent is somewhat higher, a difference that, as in the case of neurosis, may be due to a broader definition of personality disorder by the U.S. investigators or to the fact that rates of personality disorders tend to be higher in urban settings (Dohrenwend and Dohrenwend 1974a), where proportionately more of the U.S. studies were conducted.

A wide variety of different types of character and behavior problems are included under the heading of "personality disorder" in post World War II psychiatric nomenclatures. Among these, the most threatening and troublesome are antisocial or sociopathic personalities and problems of alcohol and drug addiction. These types of disorders are also least likely to be counted accurately in cross-sectional community surveys such as those we have reviewed. The reason, as

TABLE 3.9

Ranges and Medians of Rates for Alcoholism

Study Site	Number of Studies	Median (%)	Range (%)
N. America and Europe	14	2.38	0.58–31.00
U.S.	3	4.00	0.58–31.00
Non-U.S.	11	1.75	0.85– 4.99

Source: Compiled by the authors.

noted earlier, is that persons displaying such problems tend to move from the communities in which they were raised, get placed in jails or other institutions, and/or die young (cf. Robins 1966). It is difficult to know what portion of the personality disorders reported in these studies is of these three types or what proportions of these three types of disorders are missed in such cross-sectional investigations confined mainly to noninstitutionalized subjects.

Thirteen of the true prevalence studies reviewed in this section provided 14 estimates of rates of alcoholism in the community. The ranges and medians of these alcoholism rates for North American and European sites combined and for U.S. and non-U.S. sites separately are set out in Table 3.9. This study by Shore and his colleagues, conducted in an Indian village in the Pacific Northwest, accounts entirely for the particularly wide range of 9.58 percent to 31 percent among U.S. studies, as compared to the European and Canadian range of 0.85–4.99. However, since there are only three U.S. studies, the U.S. median is unaffected by this atypical finding for a particularly disadvantaged American minority group. The U.S. median of 4 percent is noticeably different from the non-U.S. figure of 1.75 percent. This difference may be a consequence simply of the small number of U.S. studies.

Apart from the atypical finding reported by Shore and his colleagues, these figures are well below the rate of "problem drinkers," tentatively put at 9 percent by Cahalan (1970) on the basis of a nationwide interview survey of U.S. adults over 21 years of age. However, more stringent criteria would put the figure for current alcoholism nearer 5 percent for men, among whom such problems are far more frequent than among women (Cahalan and Room 1973). Furthermore, the rate of alcoholism by RDC criteria is reported as 3 percent in the New Haven research (Weissman, Myers and Harding 1978a). Nevertheless, the rates from the surveys by Cahalan, Cisin, Crossley, and

Room of drinking behavior in the United States are sufficiently high to suggest that the U.S. median of 4 percent is a reasonable estimate.

Too few of the epidemiologic studies of true prevalence provide data on drug addiction for us to reach any estimate from that source. Moreover, whereas the major studies of drinking behavior in the general population of the United States have been conducted with adults aged 21 and over (cf. Straus 1976), the major studies of use of illicit drugs in the general population have been conducted with adolescents and young adults (Kandel 1978). Moreover, the focus in these studies is more on drug behavior than on drug addiction.

In a nationwide study of high school students, 2 percent of the respondents admitted to ever using heroin; 1 percent to using it regularly, that is, weekly or more (Johnston 1974). The proportions were similar in a follow-up one year after graduation. Robins (1974) found that although substantial portions of Vietnam veterans, about 20 percent, defined themselves as addicted to narcotics while in Vietnam, only 1 percent said they had been addicted since coming back. These rates were confirmed, moreover, by evidence from urine specimens. It seems unlikely, therefore, that drug addiction is anywhere near so prevalent as alcohol addiction in the U.S. general population.

The problem of estimating rates of antisocial personality on the basis of existing studies is even more difficult. Few of the epidemiologic studies provided the relevant breakdowns and fewer used research designs appropriate for estimating persons meeting the criteria for this diagnosis. Nevertheless, some results from two studies of childhood precursors of adult antisocial personality by Robins (1966, 1971) that were extracted from findings on her normal control subjects (Dohrenwend 1975) are sobering. Among 173 white and black control subjects selected from school records in St. Louis not to have had school problems in childhood, 8 percent were found on follow-up into adulthood 20–30 years later to meet the criteria for antisocial personality. The subjects were drawn from childhood neighborhoods that tended to be lower class and the cases of antisocial personality proved to be disproportionately concentrated among the blacks from the lowest socioeconomic backgrounds. Nevertheless, given the strong role of childhood antisocial behavior in predicting adult antisocial personality, the fact that 3 percent of the 62 white controls and 11 percent of the blacks received this diagnosis suggests that the rate of antisocial personality in adult males in our ethnically heterogeneous urban centers is not negligible.

Often, however, as Robins' data show, the syndrome of antisocial problems is mixed with alcohol and drug problems. It seems unlikely that antisocial personality contributes a large proportion of the cases independently of drug and alcohol problems which comprise the aggregated rate of personality disorders in the United States. Given the likely magnitude of the aggregated rate of alcohol addiction, drug addiction, and antisocial personality, which can hardly be less than 5 percent, it also seems unlikely that the rate of personality disorder is much under the 7 percent shown in Table 3.2.

The Overall Rate of Functional Psychiatric Disorder

As Table 3.2 showed, the average overall rate of functional psychiatric disorder is around 20 percent regardless of whether the estimate is based on the eight U.S. true prevalence studies, the 19 non-U.S. true prevalence studies, or the entire group of 27 communities involved in all of these epidemiologic studies. Interestingly, this estimate is reasonably close to the overall point prevalence rate of 25 percent with a diagnosis of any functional psychiatric disorder according to RDC criteria in the New Haven study (Weissman, Myers, and Harding 1978a). How do these estimates stand up in relation to our aforementioned analyses of whether the medians for the major subtypes are overestimates?

Our best hypotheses about these prevalence rates for periods of a few weeks to a year were as follows:

Schizophrenia	0.6–3.0 percent
Affective psychosis	0.3 percent
Neurosis	8.0–15.00 percent
Personality disorder	7.0 percent
Total	15.9–25.3 percent

Note that the range in rates for schizophrenia and for neurosis suggests that we need to arrive at a range for the brief period prevalence of overall rates of functional psychiatric disorders. If we simply add the estimates for the main types shown above separately for the more and less conservative figures for neurosis and for schizophrenia, this range is from about 16 percent to about 25 percent.

On the basis of current knowledge, it is not possible to identify the more valid estimate within this range. First, it is uncertain as to whether we should adopt a narrower or broader definition of schizophrenia. Second, the 15.0 percent rate for neuroses may be a function of overly broad definitions of these disorders in the U.S. studies or of the higher frequency of neuroses in urban areas, which were the sites of relatively more U.S. studies. This confounding of area and diagnostic practices makes this issue unresolvable at the present time. However, given existing evidence of the crossnational differences in diagnostic criteria (Cooper et al., 1972; Edwards 1977), it seems that the conservative decision at this point would be to give more weight to the lower figure.

The true prevalence studies discussed in this chapter are characterized by differing methods of data collection and often by case ascertainment methods comprised simply of clinical judgments of unknown reliability made by single investigators. Despite the enormous heterogeneity of these studies, the general consistency of certain relationships between rates within studies provides essential groundwork for epidemiologic analyses of etiologic factors. However, it is unlikely that much more will be gained from the continued accumulation of these types of field epidemiologic investigations. Future advances in studies of the prevalence and incidence of psychiatric disorders and the identification of etiologically significant variations in the frequency of these disorders will require more rigorous attention to the formulation of explicit rules of clinical judgment.

APPENDIX

Formulation of Hypotheses about the True Prevalence of Functional Psychiatric Disorders in the United States

TABLE 3A.1

True Prevalence Studies of Psychopathology Using Clinical Judgments Published in or after 1950

Types of Psychopathology	Study Site	
	U.S.	Non-U.S.
All types	Eaton and Weil 1955	Brunetti 1973
	Pasamanick, 1959, 1962	Piotrowski et al. 1966
	Trussell et al. 1965	(Ciechanov)
	Dohrenwend et al. 1971	Piotrowski et al. 1966
	Srole et al. 1962	(Plock)
	Cole et al. 1957	Primrose 1962
	Schwab and Warheit 1972	Fremming 1951
	Shore et al. 1973	Essen-Möller 1956
		Andersen 1975 (rural)
		Strotzka 1969
		Andersen 1975 (urban)
		Bjarnar et al. 1975
		Bremer 1951
		Hare and Shaw 1965 (New Adam)
		Helgason 1964
		Vaisanen 1975
		Fugelli 1975
		Hare and Shaw (Old Bute)
		Brunetti 1964
		Leighton et al. 1963
		Llewellyn-Thomas 1960
Psychoses	Shore et al. 1973	Llewellyn-Thomas 1960
	Eaton and Weil 1955	Piotrowski et al 1966 (Plock)
	Pasamanick 1959, 1962	Essen-Möller 1956
	Dohrenwend et al. 1971	Primrose 1962
	Cole et al. 1957	Bremer 1951
	Langner and Michael 1963	Piotrowski et al. 1966
		(Ciechanov)
		Brunetti 1973
		Leighton et al. 1963
		Fugelli 1975

Table 3A.1 (cont'd)

Types of Psychopathology	Study Site	
	U.S.	Non-U.S.
		Vaisanen 1975
		Hare and Shaw 1965 (New Adam)
		Brunetti 1964
		Andersen 1975 (urban)
		Fremming 1951
		Hare and Shaw 1965 (Old Bute)
		Helgason 1964
		Andersen 1975 (rural)
Schizophrenia	Shore et al. 1973	Llewellyn-Thomas 1960
	Eaton and Weil 1955	Primrose 1962
	Dohrenwend et al. 1971	Leighton et al. 1963
		Bremer 1951
		Fugelli 1975
		Brunetti 1973
		Essen-Möller 1956
		Helgason 1964
		Fremming 1951
		Brunetti 1964
		Vaisanen 1975
Affective	Shore et al. 1973	Brunetti 1964
	Eaton and Weil 1955	Brunetti 1973
	Dohrenwend et al. 1971	Vaisanen 1975
		Bremer 1951
		Llewellyn-Thomas 1960
		Essen-Möller 1956
		Leighton et al. 1963
		Primrose 1962
		Fremming 1951
		Helgason 1964
Neuroses	Eaton and Weil 1955	Brunetti 1973
	Pasamanick 1957, 1959	Essen-Möller 1956
	Shore et al. 1973	Fremming 1951
	Langner and Michael 1963	Llewellyn-Thomas 1960
	Cole et al. 1957	Bremer 1951
	Dohrenwend et al. 1971	Hare and Shaw 1965 (New Adam)
		Piotrowski et al. 1966 (Ciechanov)
		Hare and Shaw 1965 (Old Bute)

Table 3A.1 (cont'd)

Types of Psychopathology	Study Site	
	U.S.	Non-U.S.
		Piotrowski et al. 1966 (Plock)
		Andersen 1975 (rural)
		Primrose 1962
		Helgason 1964
		Brunetti 1964
		Andersen 1975 (urban)
		Vaisanen 1975 (North)
		Vaisanen 1975 (South)
		Fugelli 1975
		Leighton et al. 1963
Personality disorder	Eaton and Weil 1955	Brunetti 1973
	Dohrenwend et al. 1971	Piotrowski et al. 1966 (Ciechanov)
	Langner and Michael 1963	Primrose 1962
	Shore et al. 1973	Piotrowski et al. 1966 (Plock)
		Fugelli 1975
		Brunetti 1964
		Vaisanen 1975 (North)
		Fremming 1951
		Llewellyn-Thomas 1960
		Essen-Möller 1956
		Hare and Shaw 1965 (New Adam)
		Vaisanen 1975 (South)
		Helgason 1964
		Bremer 1951
		Hare and Shaw 1965 (Old Bute)
		Leighton et al. 1963

Source: Compiled by the authors.

TABLE 3A.2

Ranked Rates and Medians for All Types of Psychopathology and for Major Subtypes Reported in True Prevalence Studies Published in North America and Europe in or after 1950*

Type of Psychopathology by Geopolitical Area	Rate (%)	Study	Median
All types of psychopathology			
N. America and Europe	0.55	Eaton and Weil 1955	
	4.11	Brunetti 1973	
	8.33	Piotrowski et al 1966 (Ciechanov)	
	8.86	Essen-Möller 1956	
	10.58	Piotrowski et al. 1966 (Plock)	
	11.90	Fremming 1951	
	12.84	Pasamanick 1959, 1962	
	13.85	Andersen 1975 (rural)	
	14.80	Strotzka 1969	
	15.50	Primrose 1962	
	18.00	Trussell et al. 1965	
	18.95	Andersen 1975 (urban)	
	20.50	Bjarnar et al. 1975	
	20.85	Bremer 1951	
	21.79	Dohrenwend et al. 1971	20.85
	23.40	Srole et al. 1962	
	24.13	Hare and Shaw 1965 (New Adam)	
	25.51	Helgason 1964	
	27.11	Fugelli 1975	
	28.20	Vaisanen 1975	
	30.00	Cole et al. 1957	
	31.10	Schwab and Warheit 1972	
	34.73	Hare and Shaw 1965 (Old Bute)	
	39.70	Brunetti 1964	
	54.32	Leighton et al. 1963	
	55.84	Llewellyn-Thomas 1960	
	69.00	Shore et al. 1973	
U.S.	0.55	Eaton and Weil 1955	
	12.83	Pasamanick 1959, 1962	
	18.00	Trussell et al. 1965	
	21.79	Dohrenwend et al. 1971	22.60
	23.40	Srole et al. 1962	
	30.00	Cole et al. 1957	
	31.10	Schwab and Warheit 1972	
	69.00	Shore et al. 1973	

TABLE 3A.2 (cont'd)

Type of Psychopathology by Geopolitical Area	Rate (%)	Study	Median
Non-U.S.	3.67	Brunetti 1973	
	8.33	Piotrowski et al. 1966 (Ciechanov)	
	8.86	Essen-Möller 1956	
	10.58	Piotrowski et al. 1966 (Plock)	
	11.90	Fremming 1951	
	13.85	Andersen 1975 (rural)	
	14.80	Strotzka 1969	
	15.50	Primrose 1962	
	18.95	Andersen 1975 (urban)	
	20.50	Bjarnar et al. 1975	20.50
	20.85	Bremer 1951	
	24.13	Hare and Shaw 1965 (New Adam)	
	25.51	Helgason 1964	
	27.11	Fugelli 1975	
	28.20	Vaisanen 1975	
	34.73	Hare and Shaw 1965 (Old Bute)	
	39.70	Brunetti 1964	
	54.32	Leighton et al. 1963	
	55.84	Llewellyn-Thomas 1960	
Psychoses			
N. America and Europe	0.00	Shore et al. 1973	
	0.12	Eaton and Weil 1955	
	0.36	Llewellyn-Thomas 1960	
	0.56	Piotrowski et al. 1966 (Plock)	
	0.61	Essen-Möller 1956	
	0.85	Piotrowski et al. 1966 (Ciechanov)	
	0.86	Primrose 1962	
	0.88	Pasamanick 1959, 1962	
	1.02	Brunetti 1973	
	1.22	Leighton et al. 1963	
	1.47	Brunetti 1964	
	1.56	Fugelli 1975	1.56
	1.70	Vaisanen 1975	
	1.80	Hare and Shaw 1965 (New Adam)	
	2.40	Andersen 1975 (urban)	
	2.71	Fremming 1971	
	3.08	Dohrenwend et al. 1971	
	3.14	Cole et al. 1957	
	3.23	Bremer 1951	
	3.73	Hare and Shaw 1965 (Old Bute)	
	4.26	Helgason 1964	
	5.45	Andersen 1975 (rural)	
	8.30	Langner and Michael 1963	

TABLE 3A.2 (cont'd)

Type of Psychopathology by Geopolitical Area	Rate (%)	Study	Median
U.S.	0.00	Shore et al. 1973	
	0.12	Eaton and Weil 1955	
	0.35	Pasamanick 1959, 1962	1.72
	3.08	Dohrenwend et al. 1971	
	3.14	Cole et al. 1957	
	8.30	Langner and Michael 1963	
Non-U.S.	0.36	Llewellyn-Thomas 1960	
	0.56	Piotrowski et al. 1966 (Plock)	
	0.61	Essen-Möller 1956	
	0.85	Piotrowski et al. 1966 (Ciechanov)	
	0.86	Primrose 1962	
	1.02	Brunetti 1973	
	1.22	Leighton et al. 1963	
	1.47	Brunetti 1964	
	1.56	Fugelli 1975	
	1.70	Vaisanen 1975	1.56
	1.80	Hare and Shaw 1965 (New Adam)	
	2.40	Andersen 1975 (urban)	
	2.71	Fremming 1951	
	3.23	Bremer 1951	
	3.73	Hare and Shaw 1965 (Old Bute)	
	4.26	Helgason 1964	
	5.45	Andersen 1975 (rural)	
Schizophrenia			
N. America and Europe	0.00	Llewellyn-Thomas 1960	
	0.00	Shore et al. 1973	
	0.08	Eaton and Weil 1955	
	0.26	Primrose 1962	
	0.54	Leighton et al. 1963	
	0.54	Essen-Möller 1956	
	0.58	Fugelli 1975	0.59
	0.59	Brunetti 1973	
	0.78	Helgason 1964	
	0.83	Fremming 1951	
	0.88	Bremer 1951	
	1.47	Brunetti 1964	
	1.50	Vaisanen 1975	
	2.68	Dohrenwend et al. 1971	
U.S.	0.00	Shore et al. 1973	Too
	0.08	Eaton and Weil 1955	few
	2.68	Dohrenwend et al. 1971	studies

TABLE 3A.2 (cont'd)

Type of Psychopathology by Geopolitical Area	Rate (%)	Study	Median
Non-U.S.	0.00	Llewellyn-Thomas 1960	
	0.26	Primrose 1962	
	0.54	Leighton et al. 1963	
	0.54	Essen-Möller 1956	
	0.58	Fugelli 1975	
	0.59	Brunetti 1973	
	0.78	Helgason 1964	0.59
	0.83	Fremming 1951	
	0.88	Bremer 1951	
	1.47	Brunetti 1964	
	1.50	Vaisanen 1975	
Affective			
N. America and Europe	0.00	Brunetti 1964	
	0.00	Brunetti 1973	
	0.00	Vaisanen 1975	
	0.00	Shore et al. 1973	
	0.04	Eaton and Weil 1955	
	0.23	Essen-Möller 1956	0.29
	0.29	Bremer 1951	
	0.36	Llewellyn-Thomas 1960	
	0.40	Leighton et al. 1963	
	0.41	Dohrenwend et al. 1971	
	0.60	Primrose 1962	
	1.09	Fremming 1951	
	1.91	Helgason 1964	
U.S.	0.00	Shore et al. 1973	Too
	0.04	Eaton and Weil 1955	few
	0.41	Dohrenwend et al. 1971	studies
Non-U.S.	0.00	Brunetti 1964	
	0.00	Brunetti 1973	
	0.00	Vaisanen 1975	
	0.23	Essen-Möller 1956	
	0.29	Bremer 1951	0.33
	0.36	Llewellyn-Thomas 1960	
	0.40	Leighton et al. 1963	
	0.60	Primrose 1962	
	1.09	Fremming 1951	
	1.91	Helgason 1964	
Neuroses			
N. America and Europe	0.28	Eaton and Weil 1955	
	1.17	Brunetti 1973	

75

TABLE 3A.2 (cont'd)

Type of Psychopathology by Geopolitical Area	Rate (%)	Study	Median
	1.90	Fremming 1951	
	2.30	Essen-Möller 1956	
	5.11	Llewellyn-Thomas 1960	
	5.80	Hare and Shaw 1965 (New Adam)	
	6.46	Piotrowski et al. 1966 (Ciechanov)	
	6.91	Pasamanick 1959, 1962	
	7.05	Bremer 1951	
	8.18	Hare and Shaw 1965 (Old Bute)	9.38
	8.20	Piotrowski et al. 1966 (Plock)	
	8.40	Andersen 1975 (rural)	
	10.36	Helgason 1964	
	11.76	Brunetti 1964	
	13.25	Dohrenwend et al. 1971	
	13.32	Primrose 1962	
	16.55	Andersen 1975 (urban)	
	16.86	Cole et al. 1957	
	17.58	Vaisanen 1975 (North)	
	17.88	Vaisanen 1975 (South)	
	18.00	Shore et al. 1973	
	26.67	Fugelli 1975	
	40.00	Langner and Michael 1963	
	53.51	Leighton et al. 1963	
U.S.	0.28	Eaton and Weil 1955	
	6.90	Pasamanick 1957	
	13.25	Dohrenwend et al. 1971	15.06
	16.86	Cole et al. 1957	
	18.00	Shore et al. 1973	
	40.00	Langner and Michael 1963	
Non-U.S.	1.17	Brunetti 1973	
	1.90	Fremming 1951	
	2.30	Essen-Möller 1956	
	5.11	Llewellyn-Thomas 1960	
	5.80	Hare and Shaw 1965 (New Adam)	
	6.46	Piotrowski et al. 1966 (Ciechanov)	
	7.05	Bremer 1951	
	8.18	Hare and Shaw 1965 (Old Bute)	
	8.20	Piotrowski et al. 1966 (Plock)	8.30
	8.40	Andersen 1975 (rural)	
	10.36	Helgason 1964	
	11.76	Brunetti 1964	

TABLE 3A.2 (cont'd)

Type of Psychopathology by Geopolitical Area	Rate (%)	Study	Median
	13.32	Primrose 1962	
	16.55	Andersen 1975 (Urban)	
	17.58	Vaisanen 1975 (North)	
	17.88	Vaisanen 1975 (South)	
	26.67	Fugelli 1975	
	53.51	Leighton et al. 1963	
Personality disorders			
N. America and Europe	0.07	Eaton and Weil 1955	
	0.88	Brunetti 1973	
	1.03	Piotrowski et al. 1966 (Ciechanov)	
	1.32	Primrose 1962	
	1.47	Brunetti 1964	
	1.83	Piotrowski et al. 1966 (Plock)	
	1.97	Fugelli 1975	
	4.23	Dohrenwend et al. 1971	
	4.30	Vaisanen 1975 (North)	
	4.40	Fremming 1951	
	5.11	Llewellyn-Thomas 1960	4.76
	5.52	Hare and Shaw 1965 (New Adam)	
	5.97	Essen-Möller 1956	
	8.38	Vaisanen, 1975 (South)	
	9.30	Helgason 1964	
	9.59	Hare and Shaw 1965 (Old Bute)	
	9.80	Langner and Michael 1963	
	10.57	Bremer 1951	
	14.86	Leighton et al. 1963	
	36.00	Shore et al. 1973	
U.S.	0.07	Eaton and Weil 1955	
	4.23	Dohrenwend et al., 1971	
	9.80	Langner and Michael 1963	7.02
	36.00	Shore et al. 1973	
Non-U.S.	0.88	Brunetti 1973	
	1.03	Piotrowski et al. 1966 (Ciechanov)	
	1.32	Primrose 1962	
	1.47	Brunetti 1964	
	1.83	Piotrowski et al. 1966 (Plock)	
	1.97	Fugelli 1975	
	4.30	Vaisanen 1975 (North)	
	4.40	Fremming 1951	
	5.11	Llewellyn-Thomas 1960	4.76

TABLE 3A.2 (cont'd)

Type of Psychopathology by Geopolitical Area	Rate (%)	Study	Median
	5.52	Hare and Shaw 1965 (New Adam)	
	5.97	Essen-Möller 1956	
	8.38	Vaisanen 1975 (North)	
	9.30	Vaisanen 1975 (South)	
	9.59	Hare and Shaw 1965 (Old Bute)	
	10.57	Bremer 1951	
	14.86	Leighton et al. 1963	

*Wherever possible the rates reported for these studies were calculated for the adult population below age 60 or 65.
Source: Compiled by the authors.

TABLE 3A.3

Comparison of Male and Female Rates of Different Types of Psychopathology Reported in True Prevalence Studies Published in or after 1950[a]

Type of Psycho-pathology by Geopolitical area	Higher Rate for	Female Rate	Male Rate	Study	Ratio Female–Male
Psychoses					
N. America and Europe	Females	0.009	0.006[b]	Hagnell 1966	1.50
		0.70	0.53	Eaton and Weil 1955	1.32
		1.13	0.15	Essen-Möller 1956	7.53
		1.14	0.54	Primrose 1962	2.11
		1.90	1.70	Hare and Shaw 1965 (New Adam)	1.12
		1.93	1.23	Fugelli 1975	1.57
		3.64	2.85	Bremer 1951	1.28
		3.63	1.84	Fremming 1951	1.97
		5.33	3.22	Helgason 1964	1.66
	Males	0.24	0.60[c]	Pasamanick et al. 1959	0.45
		0.90	1.10	Brunetti 1973	0.82
		0.00	2.98	Brunetti 1964	—
		1.20	1.23	Leighton et al. 1963	0.98
		2.10	2.70	Andersen 1975 (urban)	0.78
		2.55	4.02	Dohrenwend et al. 1971	0.63
		3.00	4.60	Hare and Shaw 1965 (Old Bute)	0.65
		4.30	6.60	Andersen 1975 (rural)	0.65
U.S.	Females	0.70	0.53	Eaton and Weil 1955	1.32
	Males	0.30	0.60[c]	Pasamanick et al. 1959	0.50
		2.55	4.05	Dohrenwend et al. 1971	0.63
Non-U.S.	Females	0.009	0.006[b]	Hagnell 1966	1.50
		1.13	0.15	Essen-Möller 1956	7.53
		1.14	0.54	Primrose 1962	2.11
		1.90	1.70	Hare and Shaw 1965 (New Adam)	1.12
		1.93	1.23	Fugelli 1975	1.57
		3.63	1.84	Fremming 1951	1.97
		3.64	2.85	Bremer 1951	1.28
		5.33	3.22	Helgason 1964	1.66
	Males	0.00	2.98	Brunetti 1964	—
		0.90	1.10	Brunetti 1973	0.82

TABLE 3A.3 (cont'd)

Type of Psycho-pathology by Geopolitical area	Higher Rate for	Female Rate	Male Rate	Study	Ratio Female–Male
		1.20	1.23	Leighton et al. 1963	0.98
	Males	2.10	2.70	Andersen 1975 (urban)	0.78
		3.00	4.60	Hare and Shaw 1965 (Old Bute)	0.65
		4.30	6.60	Andersen 1975 (rural)	0.65
Schizophrenia N. America and Europe	Females	1.00	0.00	Leighton et al. 1963	—
		0.72	0.45	Fugelli 1975	1.60
		0.90	0.85	Bremer 1951	1.06
		0.94	0.62	Helgason 1964	1.52
		0.95	0.71	Fremming 1951	1.34
		0.97	0.15	Essen-Möller 1956	6.47
	Males	0.00	2.78	Brunetti 1964	—
		0.0046	0.0049[b]	Hagnell 1966	0.94
		0.16	0.36	Primrose 1962	0.44
		0.30	0.85	Brunetti 1973	0.35
		2.55	2.95	Dohrenwend et al. 1971	0.86
U.S.	Females				
	Males	2.55	2.95	Dohrenwend et al. 1971	0.86
Non-U.S.	Females	0.72	0.45	Fugelli 1975	1.60
		0.90	0.85	Bremer 1951	1.06
		0.94	0.62	Helgason 1964	1.52
		0.95	0.71	Fremming 1951	1.34
		0.97	0.15	Essen-Möller 1956	6.47
		1.00	0.00	Leighton et al. 1963	—
	Males	0.00	2.78	Brunetti 1964	—
		0.0046	0.0049[b]	Hagnell 1966	0.94
		0.30	0.85	Brunetti 1973	0.35
		0.36	0.16	Primrose 1962	0.44
Affective N. America and Europe	Females	0.48	0.00	Essen-Möller 1956	—
		0.55	0.22	Leighton et al. 1963	2.50
		0.98	0.18	Primrose 1962	5.44
		1.54	0.66	Fremming 1951	2.33
		2.36	1.47	Helgason 1964	1.61
		—	—[d]	Eaton and Weil 1955	—

TABLE 3A.3 (cont'd)

Type of Psycho-pathology by Geopolitical area	Higher Rate for	Female Rate	Male Rate	Study	Ratio Female–Male
	Males	0.00	0.57	Bremer 1951	—
		0.00	1.05	Dohrenwend et al. 1971	—
	Rates	0.06	0.06[b]	Hagnell 1966	1.00
	equal	0.00	0.00	Brunetti 1964	—
		0.00	0.00	Brunetti 1973	—
U.S.	Females	—	—[d]	Eaton and Weil 1955	—
	Males	0.00	1.05	Dohrenwend et al. 1971	—
Non-U.S.	Females	0.98	0.18	Primrose 1962	5.44
		0.48	0.00	Essen-Möller 1956	—
		0.55	0.22	Leighton et al. 1963	2.50
		1.54	0.66	Fremming 1951	2.33
		2.36	1.47	Helgason 1964	1.61
	Males	0.00	0.57	Bremer 1951	—
	Rates	0.06	0.06[b]	Hagnell 1966	1.00
	equal	0.00	0.00	Brunetti 1964	—
		0.00	0.00	Brunetti 1973	—
Neuroses N. America and Europe	Females	0.31	0.30	Eaton and Weil 1955	1.03
		1.22	0.85	Brunetti 1973	1.44
		2.34	1.46	Fremming 1951	1.60
		3.07	1.60	Essen-Möller 1956	1.92
		6.80	3.56[c]	Pasamanick et al. 1959	1.91
		6.90	3.20[b]	Hagnell 1966	2.16
		8.00	3.60	Hare and Shaw 1965 (New Adam)	2.22
		10.10	6.70	Andersen 1975 (Rural)	1.51
		10.30	3.99	Bremer 1951	2.58
		10.50	5.60	Hare and Shaw 1965 (Old Bute)	1.88
		13.95	6.85	Helgason 1964	2.04
		17.20	7.20	Dohrenwend et al. 1971	2.39
		18.76	5.56	Brunetti, 1964	3.37
		19.92	6.47	Primrose 1962	3.08
		23.00	10.10	Andersen 1975 (Urban)	2.28
		34.00	2.00	Shore et al. 1973	17.00
		34.13	20.23	Fugelli 1975	1.69
		61.69	43.07	Leighton et al. 1963	1.43

TABLE 3A.3 (cont'd)

Type of Psychopathology by Geopolitical area	Higher Rate for	Female Rate	Male Rate	Study	Ratio Female–Male
	Males				
U.S.	Females	0.31	0.30	Eaton and Weil 1955	1.03
		6.80	3.56[c]	Pasamanick et al. 1959	1.91
		17.20	7.20	Dohrenwend et al. 1971	2.39
		34.00	2.00	Shore et al. 1973	17.00
	Males				
Non-U.S.	Females	1.22	0.85	Brunetti 1973	1.44
		2.34	1.46	Fremming 1951	1.60
		3.07	1.60	Essen-Möller 1956	1.92
		6.90	3.20	Hagnell 1966	2.16
		8.00	3.60	Hare and Shaw 1965 (New Adam)	2.22
		10.10	6.70	Andersen 1975 (Rural)	1.51
		10.30	3.99	Bremer 1951	2.58
		10.50	5.60	Hare and Shaw 1965 (Old Bute)	1.88
		13.95	6.85	Helgason 1964	2.04
		18.76	5.56	Brunetti 1964	3.37
		19.92	6.47	Primrose 1962	3.08
		23.00	10.10	Andersen 1975 (Urban)	2.28
		34.13	20.23	Fugelli 1975	1.69
		61.69	43.07	Leighton et al. 1963	1.43
	Males				
Personality disorder N. American and					
	Females	0.047	0.046	Eaton and Weil 1955	1.02
		3.13	0.00	Brunetti 1964	—
		6.50	4.50	Hare and Shaw 1965 (New Adam)	1.44
		11.52	9.67	Bremer 1951	1.19
	Males	0.00	1.69	Brunetti 1973	—
		0.11	2.55	Primrose 1962	0.04
		0.72	3.12	Fugelli 1975	0.23
		2.94	5.85	Fremming 1951	0.17
		3.72	7.99	Essen-Möller 1956	0.47
		3.80	5.00	Dohrenwend et al. 1971	0.76
		4.95	13.56	Helgason 1964	0.36
		9.30	10.00	Hare and Shaw 1965 (Old Bute)	0.93
		11.81	18.77	Leighton et al. 1963	0.63
		—	—[d]	Gnat et al. 1964	—

TABLE 3A.3 (cont'd)

Type of Psychopathology by Geopolitical area	Higher Rate for	Female Rate	Male Rate	Study	Ratio Female–Male
U.S.	Females	0.047	0.046	Eaton and Weil 1955	1.02
	Males	3.80	5.00	Dohrenwend et al. 1971	0.76
Non-U.S.	Females	6.50	4.50	Hare and Shaw 1965 (New Adam)	1.44
		3.13	0.00	Brunetti 1964	—
		11.52	9.67	Bremer 1951	1.19
	Males	0.00	1.69	Brunetti 1973	—
		0.11	2.55	Primrose 1962	0.04
		0.72	3.12	Fugelli 1975	0.23
		2.94	5.85	Fremming 1951	0.17
		3.72	7.99	Essen-Möller 1956	0.47
		4.95	13.56	Helgason 1964	0.36
		9.30	10.00	Hare and Shaw 1965 (Old Bute)	0.93
		11.81	18.77	Leighton et al. 1963	0.63
		—	—[d]	Gnat et al. 1964	—

[a]Wherever possible the rates reported for these studies were calculated for the adult population below age 60 or 65.

[b]This study, not cited in previous tables, is a Swedish epidemiological survey reporting 10 year incidence rates for psychiatric disorders. It was omitted from prior tabulations involving comparisons of rates across studies because it does not use prevalence as the measure of disease frequency.

[c]The rates by sex for this study refer to rates for persons 15 years and older.

[d]The authors did not provide specific rates by sex, only their relative magnitude.

Source: Compiled by the authors.

TABLE 3A.4

True Prevalence Studies Published in or after 1950 Conducted in North America and Europe Reporting Highest Rates of All Types of Psychopathology in the Lowest Social Class and in Other than the Lowest Social Class

| Study Site | Studies in which Rate is Highest for | |
	Lowest Class	Other than Lowest Class
U.S.	Cole et al. 1957	Pasamanick et al. 1959
	Dohrenwend et al. 1971	
	Schwab and Warheit 1972	
	Shore et al. 1973	
	Srole et al. 1962	
Non-U.S.	Bremer 1951	Hare and Shaw 1965 (New
	Brown et al. 1977 (urban)[a]	Adam)
	Brown et al. 1977 (rural)[a]	Helgason 1964
	Fugelli 1975[b]	Llewellyn-Thomas 1960
	Gnat et al. 1964	Strotzka et al. 1966
	Gnat et al. 1964	Vaisanen 1975
	Hagnell 1966[c]	
	Hare and Shaw 1965 (Old Bute)	
	Primrose 1962	
	Leighton et al. 1963	

[a]This investigation not cited in previous tables, is a British true prevalence study reporting rates for psychiatric disorders among females only.

[b]Personal communication from the author, December 1, 1977.

[c]This Swedish epidemiological survey reported 10 year annual incidence rates for psychiatric disorders.

Source: Compiled by the authors.

TABLE 3A.5

Rates for All Types of Psychopathology Combined in Highest
and Lowest Social Classes Reported in True Prevalence
Studies Published in or after 1950 Conducted in
North America and Europe

Study Site	Maxi-mum Rate in	Low Rate (%)	High Rate (%)	Study	Ratio Low–High Class
U.S.	Lowest	—	—[a]	Cole et al. 1957	—
	class	19.64	26.15	Dohrenwend et al. 1971	1.33
		12.00	45.00	Schwab and Warheit 1972	3.75
		—	—[b]	Shore et al. 1973	—
		12.50	47.30	Srole et al. 1962	3.78
	Highest class	8.42	13.58	Pasamanick et al. 1959	0.62
Non-U.S.	Lowest	19.50	28.00	Bremer 1951	1.38
	class	6.00	23.00[c]	Brown et al. 1977 (urban)	3.80
		10.00	11.00[c]	Brown et al. 1977 (rural)	1.10
		25.00	51.00[d]	Fugelli 1975	2.04
		6.00	25.40	Gnat et al. 1964	4.23
		1.60	15.10	Gnat et al. 1964	9.44
		0.80	0.90[e]	Hagnell 1966	1.13
		17.76	21.05	Hare and Shaw 1965 (New Adam)	1.19
		18.92	19.86	Hare and Shaw 1965 (Old Bute)	1.05
		—	—[f]	Leighton et al. 1963	—
		17.95	19.62	Primrose 1962	1.09
		2.93	18.58	Vaisanen 1975	6.34
		51.30	1.40	Strotzka 1969	0.03
	Highest	26.19	32.33	Helgason 1964	0.81
	class	45.00	50.00	Llewellyn-Thomas 1960	0.90

[a]No figures given but authors reported that "four-fifths of the families in the lower social strata contained at least one mentally ill member, while less than one-half of the upper-stratum families were thus affected" (p. 395).

Table 3A.5 (cont'd)

[b]No relevant figures reported but authors stated that "a comparison of Probability Ratings . . . with both social (class) scales demonstrate a significant correlation between psychiatric disturbance and the lowest socioeconomic class" (p. 76).

[c]This investigation is a British study reporting rates of psychiatric disorders among females only.

[d]Personal communication from the author, December 1, 1977.

[e]This Swedish epidemiological study reported 10 year annual incidence rates for psyciatric disorders.

[f]Results reported in ridits rather than percentages.

Source: Compiled by the authors.

TABLE 3A.6

Rates for Psychoses in Highest and Lowest Social Classes Reported in True Prevalence Studies Published In or After 1950 Conducted in North America and Europe

Study Site	Maxi-mum Rate in	Low Rate (%)	High Rate (%)	Study	Ratio Low–High Class
U.S.	Lowest class	3.60	13.10	Langner and Michael 1963	3.64
		0.08	0.41	Pasamanick et al. 1959	5.13
	Highest class	3.20	5.90	Dohrenwend et al. 1971	0.54
	Rates approx-imately equal	—	—[a]	Cole et al. 1957	1.00
Non U.S.	Lowest class	0.56	0.92	Bremer 1951	1.64
		4.39	4.74	Helgason 1964	1.08
		—	—[b]	Leighton et al. 1963	—
		0.94	1.27	Primrose 1962	1.36

[a]The authors did not cite specific rates but noted that "in our survey the psychoses appear to be distributed fairly evenly across the entire social range" (p. 395).

[b]The authors did not provide specific rates by class. The relative magnitude of the rates was estimated from the figure on p. 291.

Source: Compiled by the authors.

TABLE 3A.7

Rates for Neuroses in Highest and Lowest Social Classes Reported in True Prevalance Studies Published in or after 1950 Conducted in North America and Europe

Study Site	Maxi-mum Rate in	Low Rate (%)	High Rate (%)	Study	Ratio Low–High Class
U.S.	Lowest	1.00	2.00[a]	Cole et al. 1957	2.00
	class	10.55	15.55	Dohrenwend et al. 1971	1.47
		6.25	8.01	Pasamanick et al. 1959	1.28
	Highest class	30.00	49.30	Langner and Michael 1963	0.61
Non-U.S.	Lowest class	50.50	70.00[b]	Leighton et al. 1963	1.39
		1.10	17.10	Vaisanen 1975	15.55
	Highest class	4.40	6.74	Bremer 1951	0.65
		10.14	12.42	Helgason 1964	0.82
		13.24	15.47	Primrose 1962	0.86

[a]The authors stated that "the psychoneuroses were approximately twice as frequent in the lower level families as in the upper level families" (p. 395).

[b]Figures are for symptom patterns that may not be cases.

Source: Compiled by the authors.

TABLE 3A.8

Rates for Personality Disorders in Highest and Lowest Social Classes Reported in True Prevalence Studies Published in or after 1950 Conducted in North America and Europe

Study Site	Maximum Rate in	Low Rate (%)	High Rate (%)	Study	Ratio Low–High Class
U.S.	Lowest class	0.00	6.65	Dohrenwend et al. 1971	—
		4.50	14.90	Langner and Michael 1963	3.31
	Highest class				
Non-U.S.	Lowest class	7.49	11.17	Bremer 1951	1.49
		13.23	14.50	Leighton et al. 1963	1.10
		2.48	5.11	Primrose 1962	2.06
	Highest class	9.56	10.65	Helgason 1964	0.90

Source: Compiled by the authors.

TABLE 3A.9

Ranked Rates and Medians for Alcoholism Reported in North American and European True Prevalence Studies Published in or after 1950

Geopolitical Area	Study Rate (percent)	Median
N. America and Europe	0.58 Dohrenwend et al. 1970	
	0.85 Piotrowski et al. 1966 (Ciechanov)	
	1.00 Primrose 1962	
	1.10 Fugelli 1975	
	1.17 Brunetti 1973	
	1.48 Fremming 1951	
	1.75 Piotrowski et al. 1966 (Plock)	2.38
	3.00 Vaisanen 1975	
	3.80 Brunetti 1964	
	4.00 Cole et al. 1957	
	4.21 Leighton et al. 1963	
	4.49 Helgason 1964	
	4.99 Bremer 1951	
	31.00 Shore et al. 1973	
U.S.	0.58 Dohrenwend et al. 1970	
	4.00 Cole et al. 1957	4.00
	31.00 Shore et al. 1973	
Non-U.S.	0.85 Piotrowski et al. 1966 (Ciechanov)	
	1.00 Primrose 1962	
	1.10 Fugelli 1975	
	1.17 Brunetti 1973	
	1.48 Fremming 1951	
	1.75 Piotrowski et al. 1966 (Plock)	1.75
	3.00 Vaisanen 1975	
	3.80 Brunetti 1964	
	4.21 Leighton et al. 1963	
	4.49 Helgason 1964	
	4.99 Bremer 1951	

Source: Compiled by the authors.

NOTES

1. M. Kramer, *Population Changes and Schizophrenia, 1970–1985*. Presented at the Second Rochester International Conference on Schizophrenia. Rochester, New York, May 1976. Available from Dr. Morton Kramer, Department of Mental Hygiene, 615 North Wolfe Street, Baltimore, Maryland 21205.

2. R. L. Spitzer, J. Endicott, and E. Robins, *Research Diagnostic Criteria (RDC) for a Selected Group of Functional Disorders*. June 15, 1977. Available from Dr. Robert Spitzer, Biometrics Research, New York State Psychiatric Institute, 722 West 168 Street, New York, New York 10032.

3. M. M. Weissman, J. K. Myers and P. S. Harding. 1978a. Supplementary unpublished tables for the article "Psychiatric disorders in a United States Urban Community: 1975–76." 1978. *American Journal of Psychiatry* 135: 459–62. Available from Dr. M. M. Weissman, Yale University School of Medicine, Department of Psychiatry; Depression Research Unit, Connecticut Mental Health Center, 904 Howard Avenue, Suite 2A, New Haven, Conn. 06519.

REFERENCES

Andersen, T. 1975. Physical and mental illness in a Lapp and Norwegian population. *Acta Psychiatrica Scandinavica*, suppl. 263: 47–56.

Babigian, H. M. 1975. Schizophrenia: epidemiology. In A. M. Freedman, H. I. Kaplan, and B. J. Sadock (Eds.), *Comprehensive Textbook of Psychiarty* 2. Baltimore: William and Wilkins.

Bjarner, E., Reppesgaard, H., and Astrup, C. 1975. Psychiatric morbidity in Berlevag. *Acta Psychiatrica Scandinavica*, suppl. 62.

Bremer, J. 1951. A social psychiatric investigation of a small community in northern Norway. *Acta Psychiatrica et Neurologica Scandinavica*, suppl. 62.

Brunetti, P. M. 1964. A prevalence survey of mental disorders in a rural commune in Vaucluse: methodological considerations. *Acta Psychiatrica Scandinavica* 40: 323–58.

———. 1973. Prévalence des troubles mentaux dans une population rurale du Vaucluse: données nouvelles et recapitulatives. *L'Hygiène Mentale*, 62, 1–15.

———. 1975. Rural Vaucluse: Two surveys on the prevalence of mental disorders: Summary of data. *Acta Psychiatrica Scandinavica*. 51. suppl. 263, 12–15.

Cahalan, D. 1970. *Problem Drinkers: A National Survey*. San Francisco: Jossey-Bass.

Cahalan, D., and Room, R. 1973. *Problem Drinking among American Men*. New Brunswick, N.J.: Rutgers Center of Alcohol Studies (Monograph No. 7).

Cole, N. J., Branch, C. H. H., and Orla, M. 1957. Mental illness. *A M A Archives of Neurology and Psychiatry*, 77: 393–8.

Cooper, J. E., Kendell, R. E., Gurland, B. J., Sharpe, L., Coperland, J. R. M., and Simon, R. 1972. *Psychiatric Diagnosis in New York and London*. New York: Oxford University Press.

Dohrenwend, B. P. 1975. Sociocultural and social-psychological factors in the genesis of mental disorders. *Journal of Health and Social Behavior*, 16: 365–92.

Dohrenwend, B. P., and Dohrenwend, B. S. 1969. *Local Status and Psychological Disorder: A Casual Inquiry*. New York: Wiley.

_____. 1974a. Social and cultural influences on psychopathology. *Annual Review of Psychology* 25: 417–52.

_____. 1974b. Psychiatric disorders in urban settings. In Silvano Arieti (Ed.), *American Handbook of Psychiatry*, Vol. 2, 2nd ed. New York: Basic Books, 424–47.

_____. 1976. Sex Differences and psychiatric disorder. *American Journal of Sociology*, 81: 1447–54.

Dohrenwend, B. P., Egri, G., and Mendelsohn, F. S. 1971. Psychiatric disorder in general populations: a study of the problem of clinical judgment. *American Journal of Psychiatry*, 127: 1304–12.

Dunham, H. W. 1965. *Community and Schizophrenia: An Epidemiological Analysis*. Detroit, Mich.: Wayne State University Press.

Eaton, J. W., and Weil, R. J. 1955. *Culture and Mental Disorders*. Glencoe, Ill.: Free Press.

Edwards G. 1977. Cross-national differences in measures of psychiatric morbidity. *Mental Health and Society*, 4, 126–35.

Essen-Möller, E. 1956. Individual traits and morbidity in a Swedish rural population. *Acta Psychiatrica et Neurologica Scandinavica*, suppl. 100.

Fremming, K. H. 1951. *The Expectation of Mental Infirmity in a Sample of the Danish Population*. London: Eugenics Society.

Fugelli, A. R. 1975. Mental health and living conditions in a fishing community in northern Norway. *Acta Psychiatrica Scandinavica*, suppl. 263, 39–42.

Gnat, T., Henisz, J. Sarapata, A. 1964. A Psychiatric-Socio-Statistical Study of Two Polish Towns. Presented at 1st Int. Congr. Soc. Psychiat., London.

Hagnell, O. 1966. *A Prospective Study of the Incidence of Mental Disorder*. Stockholm: Svenska Bokförlaget Norstedts–Bonniers.

Hare, E. H., and Shaw, G. K. 1965. *Mental Health on a New Housing Estate*. New York: Oxford University Press.

Helgason, T. 1964. Epidemiology of mental disorders in Iceland. *Acta Psychiatrica Scandinavica*, suppl. 173.

Hollingshead, A. B., and Redlich, F. C. 1958. *Social Class and Mental Illness: A Community Survey*. New York: Wiley.

Johnston, L. D. 1974. Drug use during and after high school: Results of a national longitudinal study. *American Journal of Public Health*, suppl., 29–37.

Kandel, D. B. Convergences in prospective longitudinal surveys of drug use in normal populations. In D. B. Kandel (Ed.), *Longitudinal Research on Drug Use*. Washington, D. C. Hemisphere-Wiley, 1978.

Kety, S. S., Rosethal, D., Wender, P. H., and Schulsinger, F. 1976. Studies based on a total sample of adopted individuals and their relatives: why they were necessary, what they demonstrated and failed to demonstrate. *Schizophrenia Bulletin* 2: 413–28.

Kringlen, E. 1976. Twins—still our best method. *Schizophrenia Bulletin* 2: 429–33.

Langner, T. S., and Michael, S. T. 1963. *Life Stress and Mental Health*. Glencoe, New York: Free Press.

Leighton, D. C., Harding, J. S., Macklin, D. B., Macmillan, A. M., and Leighton, A. H. 1963. *The Character of Danger*. New York: Basic Books.

Llewellyn-Thomas, E. 1960. The prevalence of psychiatric symptoms within an island fishing village. *Canadian Medical Association Journal*, 83: 197–204.

Pasamanick, B. 1962. A survey of mental disease in an urban population. 6 An approach to total prevalence by age. *Mental Hygiene* 46: 567–72.

Pasamanick, B., Roberts, D. W., Lemkau, D. W., and Krueger, D. B. 1959. A survey of mental disease in an urban population: prevalence by race and income. In B. Pasamanick (Ed.), *Epidemiology of Mental Disorder*. Washington, D.C. American Association for the Advancement of Society.

Piotrowski, A., Henisz, J., and Gnat, T. 1966. Individual interview and clinical examination to determine prevalence of mental disorders. *Proceedings of the Fourth World Congress of Psychiatry*, Madrid, No. 150, 2477–8.

Primrose, E. J. R. 1962. *Psychological illness: a community study*. London: Tavistock Publications.

Robins, L. N. 1966. *Deviant children grown up: a sociological and psychiatric study of sociopathic personality*. Baltimore: Williams and Wilkins.

Robins, L. N., Davis, D. H., and Nurco, D. N. 1974. How permanent was Vietnam drug addiction? *American Journal of Public Health*, suppl., 38–43.

Robins, L. N., Murphy, G. E., Woodruff, R. A., and King, L. J. 1971. Adult psychiatric status of black school boys. *Archives of General Psychiatry* 24: 338–45.

Schwab, J. J., and Warheit, G. J. January 1972. Evaluating southern mental health needs and services. *Journal of Florida Medical Association*, 17–20.

Shore, J. H., Kinzie, J. D., Hampson, J. L., and Pattison, E. M. 1973. Psychiatric epidemiology of an Indian village. *Psychiatry*, 36: 70–81.

Srole, L., Langner, T. S., Michael, S. T., Opler, M. K., and Rennie, T. A. C. 1962. *Mental Health in the Metropolis*. New York: McGraw-Hill.

Straus, R. 1976. Problem drinking in the perspective of social change, 1940–1973. In W. J. Filstead, J. J. Rossi, and M. Keller (Eds.), *Alcohol and Alcohol Problems: New Thinking and New Directions*. Cambridge, Mass.: Ballinger.

Strauss, J. S., and Gift, T. E. 1977. Choosing an approach for diagnosing schizophrenia. *Archives of General Psychiatry*, 34: 1248–53.

Strotzka, H., Leitner, I., Czerwenka-Werkstätten, G., Graupe, S. R., and Simon, M. D. 1969. *Kleinburg: Eine sozialpsychiatrische Feldstudie*. Vienna: Osterreichischer Bundesverlag für Unterricht, Wissenschaft und Kunst.

Trussell, R. E., Elinson, J., and Levin, M. L. 1956. Comparisons of various methods of estimating the prevalence of chronic disease in a community—the Hunterdon County study. *American Journal of Public Health*, 46: 173–82.

Vaisanen, E. 1975. Psychiatric disorders in Finland. *Acta Psychiatrica Scandinavica*, suppl. 263: 22–33.

Weissman, M. M., Myers, J. K. and Harding, P. S. 1978b. Psychiatric disorders in a United States urban community: 1975–76. *American Journal of Psychiatry* 135: 459–62.

Yolles, S. F., and Kramer, M. 1969. Vital statistics. In L. Bellak and L. Loeb (Eds.), *The Schizophrenic Syndrome*. New York: Grune and Stratton.

4

FORMULATION OF HYPOTHESES ABOUT THE TRUE PREVALENCE OF FUNCTIONAL AND ORGANIC PSYCHIATRIC DISORDERS AMONG THE ELDERLY IN THE UNITED STATES

Richard Neugebauer

Estimates of the true prevalence of psychiatric disorders among persons aged 60 and over are available from specialized epidemiologic studies of the elderly as well as from studies of entire adult populations. The studies that we will include in our analysis utilized clinical judgment as the basis for case identification.

Specialized field epidemiologic studies concerned exclusively with psychiatric problems of the aged began appearing in the 1950s. These investigations were prompted in part by the recognition that an increasing proportion of the population in industrialized societies belonged to this age category. They are the analogs of the specialized investigations of childhood disorders with which we began this report. Rates derived from these specialized reports have been supplemented with material from the true prevalence studies discussed in the last chapter because data in the latter studies were often arrayed in a manner that permitted extraction of age-specific rates for the elderly.

PROCEDURE OF STUDIES

Specialized true prevalence studies of the elderly, like true prevalence studies generally, adopted varying procedures for case finding and utilized somewhat different diagnostic classifications and criteria. These alternative approaches to sampling and measurement of psychopathology in the community were discussed in the last chapter and need not be repeated here. Adhering to the strategy we adopted previously, we restrict our attention to studies published in or after 1950 in order to reduce diagnostic heterogeneity across studies. However, two important departures from our previous criteria for selection and inclusion of studies should be noted.

Most of the North American and many of the European true prevalence studies of adult psychiatric disorders excluded institutionalized persons from their study populations and thereby underestimated the total rate of mental illness in society. Because the proportion of persons in the adult population under age 60 who are institutionally confined at any time is relatively small, we included these studies in arriving at our earlier estimates. We noted, however, that our estimates would tend to be on the conservative side, especially for the psychoses and personality disorders. A similar approach is less suitable for assessing mental illness rates among the elderly. Currently, approximately 5 percent of the elderly population in the United States are in mental hospitals, nursing homes, and homes for the aged, as compared to a figure of about 0.2 percent for younger adults in mental hospitals (*Psychiatric Services* 1977). Anywhere from 60 to 90 percent of the institutionalized elderly population are suffering from a severe psychiatric disorder (Berkman 1977; *Health* United States** 1977; Wang 1977). For this reason we have limited our review to true prevalence studies that included institutionalized cases in their study populations. Most specialized surveys of the elderly employed this approach in any case.

Although our earlier treatment of psychoses in the adult population under age 60 was restricted to functional disorders, no sensible estimation of psychiatric morbidity among the elderly can omit some discussion of organic psychoses. At least one-half of all admissions to psychiatric hospitals of persons over 65 in the United States are for organic psychoses (Wang 1977) and a substantial number of elderly persons living in the community are disabled by chronic organic brain syndromes severe enough to merit hospitalization (New York State Dept. of Mental Hygiene 1960; Pasamanick 1962). To keep our discussion of organic disorders within manageable limits, given the general emphasis in this volume on functional disorders, we will provide prevalence rates for senile and arteriosclerotic psychoses only, the two major forms of psychoses associated with cerebral degenerative disease.

Clinically, these disorders are usually characterized by gradual, progressive deterioration of memory, intellect, and judgment; disorganization of personality; and increasing incapacity in the normal activities of day-to-day living. With senile psychoses, this deterioration is gradual; with arteriosclerotic psychoses onset may be more rapid and of a fluctuating nature rather than an unremitting progressive decline. Several studies reported rates for severe and mild forms of these disorders. However, we examine rates for severe forms only in view of the currently recognized difficulty of distinguishing mild dementia from the occasional forgetfulness of normal senescence (Gunner-Svennson and Jensen 1976). Furthermore, because we are concerned here with the magnitude of mental health problems, we report rates for arteriosclerotic and senile psychoses together. The difficulties of differential diagnosis in this area, the apparent tendency for the two disorders to occur in association (Simon and Malamud 1965), and the fact that many studies only reported rates for the two disorders combined underscore both the value and the necessity of presenting the rates together. It should be kept in mind, therefore, when we report rates for males and for females that apparent similarities or differences in rates by sex for senile and arteriosclerotic psychoses combined might not hold if these organic disorders were considered separately.

Thirteen studies reporting rates of psychiatric disorder among the elderly were published in or after 1950. Eleven were conducted in Europe: eight in Scandinavia (Akesson 1969; Bollerup 1975; Bremer 1951; Essen-Möller 1956; Hagnell 1970; Helgason 1973; Jensen 1963; Nielsen 1962); one in France (Brunetti 1973, 1975); and two in the British Isles (Kay, Beamish, and Roth 1964; Primrose 1962). Five of these investigations were designed exclusively as specialized surveys of psychiatric morbidity among the elderly. The elderly age range for which rates were reported varies somewhat across studies. Four studies provided rates for all persons over 60; four studies considered 65 as the commencement of old age. Bollerup examined mental health among 70 year olds only; Helgason, among 74–76 year olds. Primrose arrayed his data in quinquennial tables that permitted calculation of rates for persons over 60 or 65. To maximize the number of studies we could include in this section on the elderly, we considered 60, rather than the more conventional age of 65, as marking the beginning of old age.

Only two U.S. studies provided rates for community and institutionalized cases. The work by Pasamanick et al. (1959) and Pasamanick (1962) was conducted in Baltimore in the 1950s and investigated the rate of neuroses and psychoses over the entire life-span. These rates were derived from a study of a stratified sample of subjects drawn from the Baltimore population supplemented with estimates of the rate of institutionalized cases of neuroses and psychoses based on admissions to private, public, and V.A. hospitals serving the area. This survey did not include residents of nursing homes.

The second U.S. study, launched in Syracuse, New York, by the staff of the Mental Health Research Unit of the New York State Department of Mental Hygiene (1959a, 1959b, 1960), also dates from the 1950s. (This project is conventionally referred to as the Gruenberg study after one of its principal investigators.) The Gruenberg study was concerned exclusively with the elderly and estimated rates of "psychoses of aging" based on a community survey of selected census tracts in Syracuse, combined with statistics on the rate of senile and arteriosclerotic psychoses among persons in those census tracts currently residing in mental hospitals and nursing homes. There are no relevant Canadian studies.

CENTRAL TENDENCIES IN RATES

Table 4.1 shows the number of U.S. and non-U.S. studies reporting rates for all major types of psychiatric disorder, both organic and functional, pertinent to this review. The interpretative difficulties posed by the paucity of U.S. studies are intensified by the very limited number of diagnostic categories that they investigated. In addition, the Baltimore study failed to specify the relative contribution of organic and functional psychoses to its overall rate reported for psychoses, thereby further reducing the value of its statistical findings.

The medians and ranges in rates reported across studies for each of the diagnostic headings in Table 4.1 are arrayed in Table 4.2. Separate medians and ranges of rates have been provided for U.S. as contrasted with European studies in all instances where U.S. rates were available for comparison. Only six studies, all European, reported rates for all major types of disorder under consideration here. The range in rates across these six studies is relatively narrow. We can obtain a general sense of how this European range and the median of 19.25 compares with possible U.S. rates by looking at one U.S. study that examined rates for all types of psychiatric disorder, both functional and organic, but restricted its survey to persons living in the community. Lowenthal and her colleagues (1967) conducted a field epidemiologic study using an age- and sex-stratified random sample of adults aged 60 and over living in the San Francisco area. Interview protocols were rated by project psychiatrists for levels of psychiatric impairment rather than for specific psychiatric diagnoses as in the other studies discussed in this chapter. Of the sample, 15.5 percent were considered psychiatric cases. If we assume that virtually all of the 5 percent of elderly persons who are in nursing homes, homes for the aged, or mental hospitals in the U.S. are psychiatrically impaired, the total rate for disorders among the elderly based upon the San Francisco study and the institutional data would be in the neighborhood of 20 or 21 percent. This figure approximates rather closely the European median and suggests that the U.S. overall rate may fall within the range of rates provided by the European studies.

The medians for severe arteriosclerotic and senile psychoses in the U.S. and European ranges are in reasonable agreement. Although extrapolating from just two U.S. studies is hazardous, it appears at first

TABLE 4.1

Number of True Prevalence Studies Reporting Community and Institutional Rates of Functional and/or Organic Psychiatric Disorders among the Elderly Using Clinical Judgments and Published in Europe and the United States in or after 1950

Type of Disorder	U.S. and Europe Combined		
	U.S.	Non-U.S.	Total
All major types of disorder	0	6	6
Organic psychoses			
(severe senile and severe arteriosclerotic psychoses only)	2	11	13
Major functional disorders	0	6	6
Functional psychoses	1	9	10
Schizophrenia	0	7	7
Affective	0	7	7
Neuroses*	1	9	10
Personality disorder	0	6	6

*In most studies that report rates for psychophysiological disorders this category is not mutually exclusive with neuroses. Consequently, we decided to omit specific discussion and estimation of rates for psychophysiological disorders since their inclusion would inflate unduly our estimates of overall rates of disorder.

Source: Compiled by the authors.

sight that the U.S. rates tend to fall toward the upper end of the European range. However, considerable ambiguity attends the rate of 4 percent from one of the U.S. studies. This rate comes from the Baltimore study, which, as noted earlier, on the one hand failed to specify what part of the rate for old age psychoses was comprised of organic rather than functional disorders and, on the other, did not survey nursing homes. Despite the ambiguity of the Baltimore rate, our best estimate of the rate of arteriosclerotic and senile psychoses in the United States can be stated in terms of a narrow range of rates. The lower end of the range may be set at 3.5 percent, just over the European median and about where the U.S. median would fall even if the Baltimore study's mixed rate in reality concealed a rate of zero for organic psychoses. The upper end of the range may be set at 5.5 percent, just above the U.S. median.

The range for all major functional disorders combined, like the rate for all major types of disorders generally, is based exclusively on European studies. In this context, however, the findings from the New

TABLE 4.2

Medians and Ranges of Percentages of Functional and Organic Psychiatric Disorders Combined, of Organic Disorders, of Major Types of Functional Disorders, and of Major Subtypes among the Elderly

Type of Disorder by Geopolitical Area	Number of Studies	Median	Range
All major types of disorder			
Europe	6	19.25	12.97–24.37
Organic psychoses (severe senile and severe arteriosclerotic psychoses only)			
U.S. and Europe	13	3.60	0.00 – 6.81
U.S.	2	5.41	4.00[a]– 6.81
Europe	11	3.19	0.00 – 6.81
Major functional disorders[b]			
Europe	6	14.91	9.77 –21.85
Functional psychoses			
U.S. and Europe	10	3.51	1.35 – 6.81[a]
U.S.	1	4.00	
Europe	9	3.30	1.35 – 6.81[c]
Schizophrenia			
Europe	7	0.32	0.00 – 2.22[d]
Affective			
Europe	7	1.11	0.00 – 1.36
Neuroses			
U.S. and Europe	10	6.07	1.35 –10.36
U.S.	1	7.09	
Europe	9	5.04	1.35 –10.36
Personality disorder			
Europe	6	4.90	3.27 –12.61

[a]The study reporting this rate did not indicate what proportion of the cases involved were suffering from a functional disorder and what proportion from an organic disorder.

[b]These rates include psychophysiological disorders for studies which employed mutually exclusive diagnostic categories.

[c]In European studies the rate for all functional psychoses is considerably higher than the rate that would be arrived at simply by adding "schizophrenia" and "affective illness" because a number of Scandinavian studies included under functional psychoses rates for "psychogenic psychoses."

[d]The rate forming the upper end of the range refers to males only.

Source: Compiled by the authors.

Haven Community survey using the Research Diagnostic Criteria (RDC), (Weissman, Myers, and Harding 1978a,b) discussed in the last chapter, are illuminating.[1] That community survey reported a rate of 14.4 percent for all functional disorders in persons over 65 years of age. Consider further that at least 10 percent of the 5 percent of elderly population who are in nursing homes and mental hospitals suffer from functional disorders (*Health*United States** 1977). If we add a figure for institutionalized elderly persons with functionl disorders to the New Haven rate, we obtain a rate of about 14.9 percent of functional psychiatric impairment. This U.S. rate is compatible with the range of rates reported for the European studies and close to the European median of 15 percent.

Of the two U.S. projects, only the Baltimore study provided rates for functional psychoses. However, as noted previously, this study did not stipulate what proportion of the percentage of psychoses were functional rather than organic disorders. Unfortunately, the New Haven study sheds little light on this problem because its diagnostic scheme, the RDC, does not observe the distinction between psychotic and neurotic disorders. If we attempt to reconstruct a category of functional psychoses from the RDC classification, we obtain rates ranging anywhere from 0.9 to 6.3 percent. In view of the lack of data in this area, but our aim of presenting a usefully narrow estimate of rates, the best hypothesis we can offer for the rate of functional psychoses in the elderly U.S. population is the European median of 3.5 percent.

For the sake of completeness, we have tabulated the medians and ranges of rates for schizophrenia and affective illness in European studies. However, there is little purpose in formulating specific U.S. estimates for these diagnostic subtypes given the absence of U.S. study data in this area.

The Baltimore study is again the only U.S. investigation in Table 4.2 that included rates for neuroses. The rate of 7.09 represents an underestimate because it omits persons in nursing homes. This point is underlined by findings from the New Haven community study. If we reconstruct a category of "neuroses" from four RDC categories used in this study—"minor depression," "generalized anxiety," "phobic disorder," and "panic disorder"—we obtain a rate of 4.5 percent. However, some proportion of persons considered under another category, "major depression," would probably be classified as neurotics under other diagnostic systems. The range from the New Haven study is, therefore, 4.5–9 percent and each end of the range is an underestimate in the context of this report because the study omitted institutionalized cases. These findings from the Baltimore and New Haven studies raise the possibility of a higher rate for neuroses in the U.S. elderly population than in European populations. The most sensible estimate for the U.S. rate of neuroses, which will reflect this possibility, is a range of rates with 6 percent as the lower bound and the highest rate from the European studies rounded off to 10.50.

Hypotheses concerning the frequency of personality disorders among the elderly are particularly difficult to generate because of the lack of U.S. data on this subject and the comparative breadth of the European rates. The New Haven study reported a rate of 3.6 percent for all personality disorders, which is reasonably close to the European median if we recall that institutionalized cases are omitted from the New Haven study. In the absence of any other relevant U.S. study, however, it is impossible to establish whether the New Haven rate is uncharacteristically high, uncharacteristically low, or typical. Given the intention of providing a rate that can have specific implications for mental health planning, the best current estimate for the rate of personality disorders in the U.S. elderly population would be the European median of 5 percent.

SEX DIFFERENCES

These overall estimates of prevalence for organic and functional disorders may conceal substantial variations in rates between the sexes. The analysis in the last chapter of rates by sex for specific diagnostic subtypes revealed a consistent pattern across studies of higher rates of neuroses and affective illness for females, and higher rates of personality disorder for males. In contrast, no pattern of differences emerged for functional psychoses considered together or for schizophrenia considered separately. It is of interest to explore the possibility of differences in rates in psychiatric disorders among the elderly.

Table 4.3 compares the number of studies reporting higher rates for males with those reporting higher rates for females for each disorder we have discussed. The table suggests that organic psychoses and functional psychoses do not show any consistent variations by sex. Apparently, the greater frequency of the affective psychoses among women in younger age groups no longer holds among the elderly. On the other hand, the tendency for higher rates of neuroses to be reported among females and higher rates of personality disorders to be reported among males seems to persist in the older age groups. However, these findings must be considered preliminary at best in view of the very small number of studies on which these trends are based.

TABLE 4.3

Comparison of Male and Female Rates of Senile and Arteriosclerotic Psychoses and of Functional Psychiatric Disorders among the Elderly Reported in True Prevalence Studies Published in or after 1950

Type of Psychiatric Disorder	Number of Studies in which Rate Is			Average Ratio Female–Male where One Sex Tended to Have a Higher Rate
	Higher for Males	Higher for Females	Equal	
Organic psychoses (severe senile and severe arteriosclerotic psychoses only)	5	4	1	No trend
Functional psychoses	3	4	0	No trend
Schizophrenia	1	1	3	No trend
Affective illness	1	2	1	No trend
Neuroses	1	5	0	3.35*
Personality disorder	3	1	0	0.70

*This ratio is misleadingly low since one study reported a rate of 10.30 for females but a rate of zero for males and therefore its findings could not be mathematically reflected in these calculations.

Source: Compiled by the authors.

CONCLUSION

Establishing reliable but sensibly narrow estimates of the rates of psychiatric disorders among the elderly is a difficult task because of the frequently wide range of rates reported across European studies and the paucity of U.S. investigations. Within the framework of these requirements and limitations, our present hypotheses concerning rates for psychiatric disorders in the U.S. elderly population may be summarized as follows:

Organic psychoses	3.5 percent–5.5 percent
Functional psychoses	3.5 percent
Neuroses	6.0 percent–10.5 percent
Personality disorders	5.0 percent
Total	18.0 percent–24.5 percent

Our review also suggests that these disorders are not distributed evenly by sex but that females over 60 tend to have higher rates of neuroses and males higher rates of personality disorder.

In conclusion, it should be emphasized that the estimated range for all types of psychiatric disorder among the elderly cannot be compared directly to the estimate offered at the end of the last chapter for adults under age 60. The rates for the elderly include organic psychoses whereas those for the younger adults do not. Also, the elderly rate is based primarily on studies that included institutionalized cases in their count; the true prevalence studies of younger adults generally restricted their survey to cases in the community.

APPENDIX

Formulation of Hypotheses about the True Prevalence of Functional and Organic Psychiatric Disorders among the Elderly Population in the United States

TABLE 4A.1

True Prevalence Studies Reporting Community and Institutional Rates of Functional and/or Organic Psychiatric Disorders among the Elderly Using Clinical Judgments and Published in or after 1950

Type of Disorder	North America and Europe Combined	
	U.S.	Non-U.S.
All major types of disorder		Bollerup (1975)
		Bremer (1951)
		Essen-Möller (1956)
		Helgason (1973)
		Kay et al. (1964)
		Nielsen (1962)
Organic psychoses (severe senile and arteriosclerotic psychoses only)	Gruenberg (1959)	Akesson (1969)
	Pasamanick (1959, 1962)	Bollerup (1975)
		Bremer (1951)
		Brunetti (1973, 1975)
		Essen-Möller (1956)
		Hagnell (1966, 1970)
		Helgason (1973)
		Jensen (1963)
		Kay et al. (1964)
		Nielsen (1962)
		Primrose (1962)
Major functional disorders		Bollerup (1975)
		Bremer (1951)
		Essen-Möller (1956)
		Helgason (1973)
		Kay et al. (1964)
		Nielsen (1962)
Functional psychoses in general	Pasamanick (1959, 1962)[a]	Bollerup (1975)
		Bremer (1951)
		Essen-Möller (1956)
		Hagnell (1966[a], 1970)

TABLE 4A.1 (con't.)

Type of Disorder	North America and Europe Combined	
	U.S.	Non-U.S.
Schizophrenia		Helgason (1973)
		Jensen (1963)
		Kay et al. (1964)
		Nielsen (1962)
		Primrose (1962)[b]
		Bollerup (1975)
		Bremer (1951)
		Essen-Möller (1956)
		Jensen (1963)
		Kay et al. (1964)
		Nielsen (1962)
		Primrose (1962)[b]
Affective		Bollerup (1975)
		Bremer (1951)
		Essen-Möller (1956)
		Jensen (1963)
		Kay et al. (1964)
		Nielsen (1962)
		Primrose (1962)[b]
Neuroses	Pasamanick (1959, 1962)	Bollerup (1975)
		Bremer (1951)
		Essen-Möller (1956)
		Hagnell (1966, 1970)
		Helgason (1973)
		Jensen (1963)
		Kay et al. (1964)
		Nielsen (1962)
		Primrose (1962)
Personality disorders		Bollerup (1975)
		Bremer (1951)
		Essen-Möller (1956)
		Helgason (1973)
		Kay et al. (1964)
		Nielsen (1962)

[a]This author provides prevalence rates for senile psychoses but does not specify what proportion of the disorders are functional, what proportion organic.

[b]Rates restricted to the elderly could be obtained from the tables of this report for males only.

Source: Compiled by the authors.

TABLE 4A.2

Ranked Rates, Expressed in Percentages, and Medians for
Functional and Organic Psychiatric Disorders Combined, for
Organic Disorders, for Major Types of Functional Disorders and
for Major Subtypes among the Elderly
(rates derived from true prevalence studies providing community
and institutional rates using clinical judgments and published in
Europe and North America in or after 1950)

Type of Disorder by Geopolitical Area	Study Rate		Median
All major types of disorder	12.97	Bollerup (1975)	
N. America and Europe	17.90	Nielsen (1962)	
	18.28	Essen-Möller (1956)	19.25
	20.22	Kay et al. (1964)	
	23.00	Helgason (1973)	
	24.37	Bremer (1951)	
Organic psychoses (severe senile and arteriosclerotic psychoses)			
U.S. and Europe	0.00	Brunetti (1973, 1975)	
	0.95	Akesson (1969)	
	1.10	Jensen (1963)	
	2.52	Bremer (1951)	
	3.07	Nielsen (1962)	
	3.19	Bollerup (1975)	
	3.60	Helgason (1973)	3.60
	3.60	Primrose (1962)	
	4.00[a]	Pasamanick (1959, 1962)	
	4.97	Essen-Möller (1956)	
	5.23	Kay, et al. (1964)	
	6.81[a]	Hagnell (1966, 1970)	
	6.81	Gruenbeg (1959)	
U.S.	4.00[a]	Pasamanick (1959, 1962)	5.41
	6.81	Gruenberg (1959)	
Europe	0.00	Brunetti (1973, 1975)	
	0.95	Akesson (1969)	
	1.10	Jensen (1963)	
	2.52	Bremer (1951)	
	3.07	Nielsen (1962)	
	3.19	Bollerup (1975)	3.19
	3.60	Helgason (1973)	
	3.60	Primrose (1962)	
	4.97	Essen-Möller (1956)	

TABLE 4A.2 (con't.)

Type of Disorder by Geopolitical Area	Study Rate		Median
	5.23	Kay et al. (1964)	
Major functional	6.81[a]	Hagnell (1966, 1970)[a]	
disorders	9.77	Bollerup (1975)	
Europe	13.32	Essen-Möller (1956)	
	14.83	Nielsen (1962)	
	14.98	Kay et al. (1964)	14.91
	19.40	Helgason (1973)	
	21.85	Bremer (1951)	
Functional psychoses			
U.S. and Europe	1.35	Essen-Möller (1956)	
	1.44	Bollerup (1975)	
	2.01	Jensen (1963)	
	2.44	Kay et al. (1964)	
	3.33[b]	Primrose (1962)	3.51
	3.68	Nielsen (1962)	
	3.70	Helgason (1973)	
	4.00[a]	Pasamanick (1959, 1962)	
	4.20	Bremer (1951)	
	6.81[a]	Hagnell (1966, 1970)	
U.S.	4.00[a]	Pasamanick (1957)	4.00
Europe	1.35	Essen-Möller (1956)	
	1.44	Bollerup (1975)	
	2.01	Jensen (1963)	
	2.44	Kay et al. (1964)	
	3.33[b]	Primrose (1962)	3.33
	3.68	Nielsen (1962)	
	3.70	Helgason (1973)	
	4.20	Bremer (1951)	
	6.81[a]	Hagnell (1966, 1970)	
Schizophrenia			
Europe	0.00	Bremer (1951)	
	0.00	Nielsen (1962)	
	0.00	Jensen (1963)	
	0.32	Bollerup (1975)	0.32
	0.45	Essen-Möller (1956)	
	1.08	Kay et al. (1964)	
	2.22[b]	Primrose (1962)	
Affective			
Europe	0.00	Bremer (1951)	
	0.45	Essen-Möller (1956)	
	0.48	Bollerup (1975)	
	1.11[b]	Primrose (1962)	1.11
	1.23	Nielsen (1962)	

TABLE 4A.2 (con't.)

Type of Disorder by Geopolitical Area		Study Rate	Median
	1.28	Jensen (1963)	
	1.36	Kay et al. (1964)	
Neuroses			
U.S. and Europe	1.35	Essen-Möller (1956)	
	1.47	Jensen (1962)	
	3.99	Nielsen (1962)	
	4.33	Bollerup (1975)	
	5.04	Bremer (1951)	6.07
	7.09	Pasamanick (1959, 1962)	
	8.51	Hagnell (1966, 1970)	
	8.93	Kay et al. (1964)	
	9.90	Helgason (1973)	
	10.36	Primrose (1962)	
U.S.	7.09	Pasamanick (1959, 1962)	7.09
Europe	1.35	Essen-Möller (1956)	
	1.47	Jensen (1962)	
	3.99	Nielsen (1962)	
	4.33	Bollerup (1975)	
	5.04	Bremer (1951)	5.04
	8.51	Hagnell (1966, 1970)	
	8.93	Kay et al. (1964)	
	9.90	Helgason (1973)	
	10.36	Primrose (1962)	
Personality disorder			
Europe	3.27	Nielsen (1962)	
	3.62	Kay et al. (1964)	
	3.99	Bollerup (1975)	
	5.80[c]	Helgason (1973)	4.90
	10.61	Essen-Möller (1956)	
	12.61	Bremer (1951)	

[a]This author provides rates for senile psychoses, but does not specify what proportion of the disorders are functional, what proportion organic.

[b]Rates restricted to the elderly could be obtained from the tables of this report for males only.

[c]This rate may include a few cases of mental retardation.

Source: Compiled by the authors.

TABLE 4A.3

Comparison of Male and Female Rates, Expressed in Percentages, for Senile and Arteriosclerotic Psychoses and for Different Types of Functional Psychiatric Disorders among the Elderly (rates derived from true prevalence studies providing community and institutional rates using clinical judgments and published in Europe and North America in or after 1950)

Type of Psychiatric Disorder	Higher Rate for	Female Rate	Male Rate	Study	Ratio Female–Male
Organic psychoses	Females	1.18	0.72	Akesson (1969)	1.64
(severe senile and		3.29	2.85	Nielsen (1962)	1.15
arteriosclerotic		7.20	6.40[a]	Hagnell (1966, 1970)	1.13
psychoses)		7.12	6.57	Gruenberg (1960)	1.08
	Males	2.30	2.50[b]	Helgason (1973)	0.92
		1.72	3.28	Bremer (1951)	0.52
		3.03	4.44	Primrose (1962)	0.68
		0.93	5.59	Bollerup (1975)	0.17
		3.90	6.07	Essen-Möller (1956)	0.64
	Equal rates	0.00	0.00	Brunetti (1973, 1975)	—
Functional psychoses	Females	2.18	0.47	Essen-Möller (1956)	4.64
		5.97	1.41	Nielsen (1962)	4.23
		7.20	6.40[a]	Hagnell (1966, 1970)[a]	1.13
		5.17	3.28	Bremer (1951)	1.58
	Males	1.24	1.64	Bollerup (1975)	0.76
		4.90	5.10	Helgason (1973)[b]	0.96
		—	—	Primrose (1962)[c]	—
Schizophrenia	Females	0.87	0.00	Essen-Möller (1956)	—
	Males	0.31	0.33	Bollerup (1975)	0.94
	Equal rates	0.00	0.00	Bremer (1951)	—
		0.00	0.00	Nielsen (1962)	—
				Primrose (1962)[d]	—

TABLE 4A.3 (con't.)

Type of Psychiatric Disorder	Higher Rate for	Female Rate	Male Rate	Study	Ratio Female–Male
Affective illness	Females	0.87	0.00	Essen-Möller (1956)	—
		1.65	0.81	Nielsen (1962)	2.04
	Males	0.00	0.99	Bollerup (1975)	—
	Equal rates	0.00	0.00	Bremer (1951)	—
Neuroses	Females	10.30	0.00	Bremer (1951)	—
		7.45	0.99	Bollerup (1975)	7.53
		5.14	2.85	Nielsen (1962)	1.80
		15.15	3.33	Primrose (1962)	4.55
		11.08	5.81	Hagnell (1966, 1970)	1.91
	Males	1.31	1.40	Essen-Möller (1956)	0.94
Personality disorder	Females	4.66	3.29	Bollerup (1975)	1.42
	Males	2.47	4.07	Nielsen (1962)	0.61
		3.07	13.08	Essen-Möller (1956)	0.23
		8.60	16.39	Bremer (1951)	0.52

[a]This author provides rates for senile psychoses but does not specify what proportion of the disorders are functional, what proportion organic.

[b]Cumulative incidence for the elderly population of this study from ages 61 to 74.

[c]It is possible to extrapolate from the tables presented in this study that the rate of functional psychoses among males exceeded that among females. However, the exact rates could not be calculated.

[d]It is possible to extrapolate from the tables presented in this study that the rate of schizophrenia among males was either equal to or exceeded the rate among females. However, the exact rates could not be calculated.

Source: Compiled by the authors.

NOTES

1. M. M. Weissman, J. K. Myers and P. S. Harding 1978a. Supplementary unpublished tables for the article "Psychiatric disorders in a United States Urban Community: 1975–76." 1978. American Journal of Psychiatry, 135, 459–62. Available from Dr. M. M. Weissman, Yale University School of Medicine, Department of Psychiatry; Depression Research Unit, Connecticut Mental Health Center, 904 Howard Avenue, Suite 2A, New Haven, Conn. 06519.

REFERENCES

Akesson, H. O. 1969. A population study of senile and arteriosclerotic psychoses. *Human Heredity* 19: 546–66.

Berkman, B. 1977. Community mental health services for the elderly. *Community Mental Health Review* 2, No. 3: 1–9.

Bollerup, T. Rinder. 1975. Prevalence of mental illness among 70-year olds domiciled in nine Copenhagen suburbs. *Acta Psychiatrica Scandinavica* 51: 327–39.

Bremer, J. 1951. A social psychiatric investigation of a small community in northern Norway. *Acta Psychiatrica et Neurologica Scandinavica*, suppl. 62.

Brunetti, P. M. 1973. Prévalence des troubles mentaux dans une population rurale du Vaucluse: données nouvelles et recapitulatives. *L'Hygiène Mentale* 62: 1–15.

———. 1975. Rural Vaucluse: Two surveys on the prevalence of mental disorders: Summary of data. *Acta Psychiatrica Scandinavica* 51, suppl. 263: 12–15.

Essen-Möller, E. 1956. Individual traits and morbidity in a Swedish rural population. *Acta Psychiatrica et Neurologica Scandinavica*, suppl. 100.

Gunner-Svensson, F., and Jensen, K. 1976. Frequency of mental disorders in old age. *Acta Psychiatrica Scandinavica* 53: 283–97.

Hagnell, O. 1966. *A Prospective Study of the Incidence of Mental Disorder.* Stockholm: Svenska Bokförlaget Norstedts—Bonniers.

———. 1970. Disease expectancy and incidence of mental illness among the aged. *Acta Psychiatrica Scandinavica* 46, suppl. 219: 83–9.

Health* United States* 1976–1977. 1977. DHEW, Public Health Service, Health Resources Administration, National Center for Health Statistics, National Center for Health Services Research. DHEW Publication No. (HRA) 77–1232.

Helgason, T. 1973. Epidemiology of mental disorders in Iceland: a geriatric follow-up. In R. de la Fuente and M. Weissman (Eds.), *Proceedings of the Fifth World Congress of Psychiatry, Mexico, 1971*, Excerpta Med. (Amst.) Sect. VIIIB.

Jensen, K. 1963. Psychiatric problems in four Danish old age homes. *Acta Psychiatrica Scandinavica*, suppl. 169: 411–19.

Kay, D. W. C., Beamish, P., and Roth, M. 1964. Old age mental disorders in Newcastle-upon-Tyne. Part I. A study of prevalence. *British Journal of Psychiatry* 110: 146–58.

Lowenthal, M. F., Berkman, P. L., Brisette, G. G., Buehler, J. A., Pierce, R. C., Robinson, B. C., and Trier, M. L. 1967. *Aging and Mental Disorders in San Francisco: A Social Psychiatric Study.* San Francisco: Jossey-Bass.

New York State Department of Mental Hygiene, Staff of the Mental Health Research Unit. 1959a. A mental health survey of older people. 1. *Psychiatric Quarterly* 33, Part 1, 45–99.

———. 1959b. A mental health survey of older people. 2. *Psychiatric Quarterly* 33, Part 2, 252–300.

———. 1960. A mental health survey of older people. 3. *Psychiatric Quarterly* 34, Part 1, 34–75.

Nielsen, J. 1962. Geronto-psychiatric period-prevalence investigation in a geographically delimited population. *Acta Psychiatrica Scandinavica* 38: 307–30.

Pasamanick, B. 1962. A survey of mental disease in an urban population. 6. An approach to total prevalence by age. *Mental Hygiene*, 46, 567–72.

Pasamanick, B., Roberts, D. W., Lemkau, D. W., and Krueger, D. B. 1959. A survey of mental disease in an urban population: prevalence by race and income. In B. Pasamanick (Ed.) *Epidemiology of Mental Disorder.* Washington, D.C.: American Association for the Advancement of Society.

Primrose, E. J. R. 1962. *Psychological Illness: A Community Study.* London: Tavistock Publications.

Psychiatric Services and the Changing Institutional Scene, 1950–1985. 1977. DHEW Public Health Service, National Institute of Mental Health. Series B, No. 12 ADAMHA. DHEW Publication No. (ADM) 77–433.

Simon, A., and Malamud, N. 1965. Comparison of clinical and neuropathological findings in geriatric mental illness. In *Psychiatric Disorders in the Aged.* Manchester: Geigy.

Wang, H. S. 1977. Dementia of old age. In W. Lynn Smith and M. Kinsbourne (Eds.), *Aging and Dementia.* New York: Spectrum Publications, pp. 1–24.

Weissman, M. M., Myers, J. K., and Harding, P. S. 1978b. Psychiatric disorders in a U.S. urban community: 1975–76. *American Journal of Psychiatry* 135: 459–62.

5

FORMULATION OF HYPOTHESES ABOUT THE TRUE PREVALENCE OF DEMORALIZATION IN THE UNITED STATES

Bruce Link
Bruce P. Dohrenwend

Strongly influenced by the work of the U.S. Army Research Branch on psychiatric screening during World War II (Star 1951a, 1950b), a growing number of investigators, mainly in the United States, have used small batteries of symptom questions with fixed alternative response formats in epidemiologic studies of psychiatric disorder conducted since 1950. Typically, such batteries include questions about a variety of physical and psychological symptoms thought to be related to psychiatric disorders. The respondent is asked to reply to items such as, "You feel anxiety about something or someone almost all the time," with response alternatives of true or false, or, "Have you ever been bothered by 'cold sweats'? Would you say often, sometimes, or never?" A number of brief screening scales incorporating such questions were developed (e.g., Brodman et al. 1952; Dupuy 1974; Goldberg 1972; Gurin, Veroff, and Feld 1960; Langner 1962; Macmillan 1957) and used to measure such diverse constructs as "mental health," "mental illness," "psychiatric disorders," "emotional adjustment," "symptoms of stress," and "psychophysiological symptoms" (Seiler 1973, p. 257).

Although these scales have been repeatedly criticized for lack of validity (Crandell and Dohrenwend 1967; Dohrenwend 1966; Dohrenwend 1973; Dohrenwend and Dohrenwend 1969; Phillips and Clancy 1972; Seiler 1973; Tousignant and Lachapelle 1974; and notes 1–3), they continue to be used at least in part because of their obvious advantage of economy in time, money and skill, ease of administration, and ease of data handling. It is now clear, however, that such measures are very imperfectly and often only indirectly related to clinical psychiatric disorders (Dohrenwend 1973; and notes 4–7).

RELATION OF THE SCREENING SCALES TO
CLINICAL PSYCHIATRIC DISORDER

Several studies (Dohrenwend 1973; Langner 1962; note 8) used both screening scales and clinical judgments to identify psychiatric cases in the same samples of respondents from the general population. The diagrams presented in Figure 5.1 are generated from these studies and clearly illustrate the imperfect relationship between the two procedures. In all three studies the proportion of cases identified by both procedures is less than half of all cases identified by one or both. Furthermore, the fact that the psychiatrists in the Dohrenwend and Langner studies had the information from the screening scales on hand when they made the clinical judgments may have inflated the overlap between the two assessments. In the Myers and Weissman study, where the judgments were made without knowledge of responses to the screening scale, the overlap is only 31 percent. In summary, these three studies show that the relationship between screening scale results and clinical evaluations is highly imperfect.

WHAT THE SCREENING SCALES MEASURE: THE
CONSTRUCT OF DEMORALIZATION

Fortunately, there is a plausible hypothesis as to what these scales are in fact measuring. Dohrenwend and his colleagues (note 9) found that several of these screening scales were highly correlated with measures of self-esteem, helplessness–hopelessness, sadness, and anxiety, all of which are major facets of what Jerome Frank called "demoralization" (1973). Frank posited that this condition, although only indirectly related to clinical psychiatric disorder, is a major factor in leading people to seek help and "the common property of the conditions that psychotherapy attempts to relieve" (Frank 1973, p. 278). In Frank's theoretical formulation as well as in relevant research reviewed by Dohrenwend and his colleagues (note 10), demoralization is a condition that is likely to be experienced in association with a variety of problems including severe physical illness, particularly chronic illness, stressful life events, psychiatric disorders, and perhaps conditions of social marginality as experienced by minority groups and persons such as housewives and the poor whose social positions block them from mainstream strivings.

Information as to the prevalence of demoralization in the population at large and within subgroups is, we believe, of major importance. If Frank is right, even in the absence of clinical psychiatric disorder

FIGURE 5.1

Relation of clinical disorder to screening scale results.

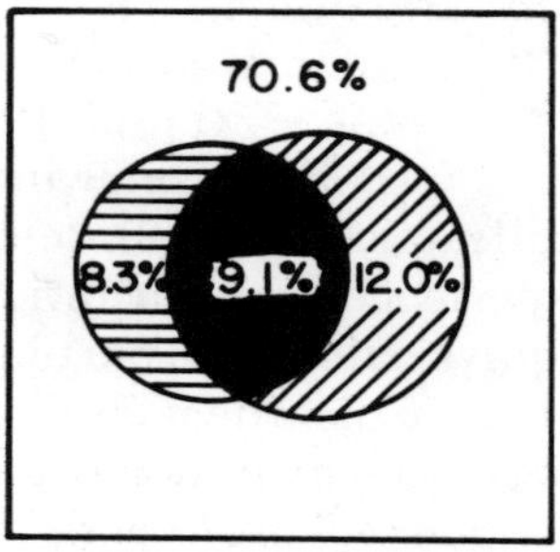

		CLINICAL DISORDER	SCREENED AS A CASE	N	%
LANGNER (1962) 22-ITEM	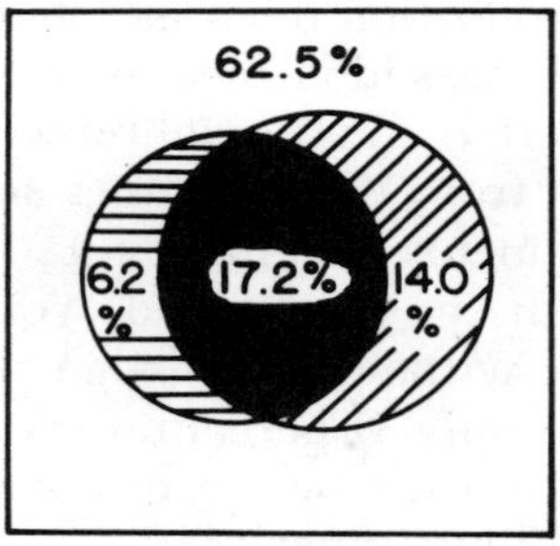 62.5% (6.2% 17.2% 14.0%)	YES	YES	286	17.2
		NO	YES	233	14.0
		YES	NO	103	6.2
		NO	NO	1,038	62.5
DOHRENWEND (1973) 22-ITEM	59.7% (5.6% 16.9% 17.7%)	YES	YES	21	16.9
		NO	YES	22	17.7
		YES	NO	7	5.6
		NO	NO	74	59.7
MYERS + WEISSMAN (NOTE 5) GURIN	70.6% (8.3% 9.1% 12.0%)	YES	YES	46	9.1
		NO	YES	61	12.0
		YES	NO	42	8.3
		NO	NO	358	70.6

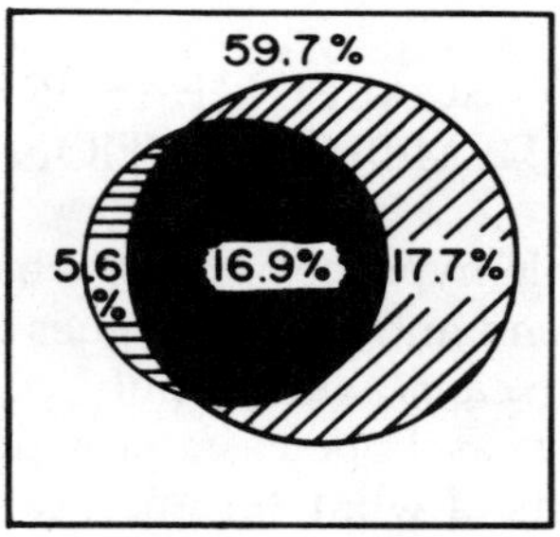

SCREENED & CLINICAL ■   SCREENED ONLY ▨   CLINICAL ONLY ▤   NEITHER

Source: Constructed by the authors.

demoralization is a significant factor in leading individuals to seek treatment from mental health professionals (note 11). Moreover, it should be viewed as an important indicator of distress within the population, and within various subgroups, because it can exacerbate the impairment and suffering accompanying a wide variety of problems, including those of coping with both severe physical illness and psychotic symptomatology. Before proceeding to report the findings on demoralization, a brief methodological note will be presented to explain the criteria employed for including a screening scale as a measure of demoralization.

EQUIVALENCE OF VARIOUS SCREENING SCALES

Much of the evidence linking screening scales to the concept of demoralization is presented in a paper by Dohrenwend et al. (note 12). This analysis linked the Langner 22-item psychiatric screening index (Langner 1962) and the Health Opinion Survey (HOS) (Macmillan 1957) to demoralization. But these two scales do not exhaust the field of scales that may measure demoralization. In order to assess whether scales such as the Gurin (Gurin, Veroff, and Feld 1960), the General Well Being Scale (GWB) (Dupuy 1974), the Center for Epidemiological Studies Depression scale (CES-D) (Radloff 1977), the Symptom Check List-90 (SCL-90) (Derogatis, Lipman, and Covi 1973), and others also measure demoralization, it was decided that the evidence should indicate that they share most if not all of their reliable variance with the Langner and HOS scales. In the absence of compelling empirical evidence placing a scale on the demoralization dimension the decision was made not to include studies using the scale in the analysis to be presented despite face validity linking the scale to demoralization.

The evidence required to make these decisions consisted of the internal consistency reliability of each of the scales and the intercorrelations between scales. In our search of the literature we found studies that provided the necessary information to test whether the GWB, CES-D, and SCL-90 scales should be included on the demoralization dimension. Six studies were found that provided the relevant information (Radloff 1977; Weissman et al. 1977; notes 13–16). The analyses based on this information are presented in Table 5.1. First, the correlations between scales were corrected for attenuation to determine the extent to which scales shared reliable variance. We are aware that correction for attenuation is sometimes criticized as an inappropriate way of making relationships between inadequate measures appear stronger than they are. However, our use of corrected correlations

TABLE 5.1

Reliability Coefficients of Screening Scales and Correlations between Scales

| Source | Scale | Scale | | | | |
		Langner	NOS	CES-D	GWB	SCL-90
Radloff (1977)	Langner	.80		.54		
Mueller[a]	Langner	.80			−.76	
Edwards et al.	Langner	.80			−.64	.53
Husaini & Neff [b]	HOS		.85[c]	.48	−.67	
Warheit[d]	HOS		.81			
Radloff (1977)	CES-D	.66		.85		
Husaini & Neff [b]	CES-D		.56	.87[c]	−.62	
Weissman et al. (1977)	CES-D			.86[e]		.72
						.84
Husaini & Neff [b]	GWB		−.76	−.70	.91[c]	
Edwards et al.	GWB	−.74			.95	−.72
Mueller[a]	GWB	−.88			−.93[e]	
Edwards et al.	SCL-90	.61			−.76	.95
Weissman et al. (1977)	SCL-90			.80		.95[e]
				.93		

[a] D. Mueller, personal communication.
[b] B. Husaini and J. Neff, personal communication.
[c] Calculated by B. Link.
[d] G. Warheit, personal communication.
[e] No internal consistency reliability figure reported; mean of available figures used in correcting for attenuation.
Source: Compiled by the authors.

does not involve interpreting the absolute magnitudes of the correlations but, instead, their magnitudes relative to other correlations. By correcting for attenuation we eliminated the effect of differences in the reliability of the scales on the relative magnitudes of their correlations.

When we examined the corrected correlations and the content of the scales associated with them, we noted that the questions in the scales were keyed to different time periods, ranging from "in the past week" to "ever," and that the greater the time difference between scales the lower the correlation between them. Thus, the SCL-90 and the CES-D both ask respondents about symptoms in the past week and their correlation, corrected for attenuation, is as high as .93 (Weissman et al. 1977). In contrast, the correlation between the CES-D and the HOS, in which questions refer to "ever" or "in general," is .56 (note 17), again after correction.

Because of this problem a regression equation was computed using the time difference between scales as a predictor of the variation in the magnitude of correlations between scales. This equation, which explains 54 percent of the variance in the correlations, gives strong support to the idea that a method factor, the time difference between scales, reduces scale correlations. It suggests that if there were no time difference between tests the mean correlation between scales that differ in time keying from "in the past week" to "ever" would be increased by 19.2 and that the mean of those differing by one time step should be increased by 9.6. Though we recognize that there are methodological problems involved in predicting individual scores, we have used the computed regression equation to estimate, for illustrative purposes, what the correlations between scales would be if there were no time difference between them. We did this by adding the appropriate correction factor, either 19.2 or 9.6 depending on the time difference between scales, to the actual correlation corrected for attenuation. The results are shown in Table 5.2.

Although all of the scales appear to be highly interrelated and to share a sizable portion of variation in common, the evidence argues most strongly for including the GWB in the demoralization dimension. The SCL-90 and CES-D, though highly related to the demoralization dimension, seemed more highly related to one another than to the Langner and HOS scales. When this evidence had been interpreted conservatively it was decided to include GWB studies but not studies using the CES-D or SCL-90. Thus, pending future research clarifying the issues of method involved it was decided to include studies using the Langner 22-item, the HOS, and the GWB as indicators of demoralization.

FORMULATION OF HYPOTHESES ABOUT RATES OF DEMORALIZATION IN THE UNITED STATES

Data from studies that have assessed the prevalence of demoralization, thus defined, are summarized in Table 5.3. As noted, all were conducted in the United States after 1950. The percentages refer to

TABLE 5.2

Best Estimates of Correlations between Scales if Their Questions Were Keyed for the Same Time Period

Scales	Time Difference	Best Estimate Correlation
Langner with CES-D (Radloff 1977)	3	.852
Langner with GWB (Mueller[a])	2	−.976
Langner with GWB (Edwards et al.)	3	−.932
Langner with SCL-90 (Edwards et al.)	3	.802
HOS with CES-D (Husaini and Neff [b])	3	.752
HOS with GWB (Husaini and Neff [b])	2	−.856
CES-D with SCL-90 (Weissman et al. 1977)	1	.800
CES-D with SCL-90 (Weissman et al. 1977)	1	.930
GWB with CES-D (Husaini and Neff [b])	2	−.796
GWB with SCL-90 (Edwards et al.)	1	−.760

[a] D. Mueller, personal communication.
[b] B. Husaini and J. Neff, personal communication.
Source: Compiled by the authors.

Time difference: 1 = same time reference
2 = either a difference from "ever" to "past month" or from "past month" to "past week"
3 = difference of "ever" to "past week"

people who scored above a cutoff point that the author of the study considered indicative of a sufficient degree of psychological distress to be considered a "case." In addition, in each instance the cutoff point suggested by the author was supported by evidence, either his or her own, or evidence presented elsewhere in the literature, indicating that psychiatric patients were discriminated from nonpatients with some degree of regularity at that cutoff point. With the aim of developing hypotheses about the prevalence of demoralization in the United States population as a whole and in various subgroups we have presented medians summarizing the results of relatively local community studies and the actual results reported for two nationwide studies.

Overall Rate

The 14 local community studies (listed in the Appendix), which were conducted since 1950 and meet the various criteria mentioned above,

TABLE 5.3

Estimates of the Prevalence of Demoralization Based on Studies Conducted in the United States Since 1950 (Numbers of studies on which medians are based in parentheses)

Source	Total samples	Percent demoralized					
		Males	Females	Lowest class	Highest class	Rural	Urban
Local community studies-median	24.5(14)	21.7(5)	32.2(5)	31.4(5)	9.2(5)	16.6(3)	25.3(7)
Nationwide studies							
Dupuy	25.9	20.1	30.8	38.6	17.0		
NORC[a]	31.8	26.8	35.5	49.7	18.4		

[a]NORC data were made available by the study director, Eleanor Singer, and analyzed by Bruce Link.
Source: Compiled by the authors.

were done in different regions of the United States in varying urban and rural contexts, and often using different cutoff points and sampling procedures. At the same time, the two nationwide studies have procedural idiosyncracies of their own including variation in the instrument used, the cutoff point adopted, and the time keying of questions, to name a few. Therefore, the estimate of 24.5 percent demoralized based on the median of the 14 local community studies could be biased in its sampling by failing to represent some regions within the United States but controls, to some extent, for the difference in methods by taking the central tendency of their estimates. In contrast, the Dupuy (1974) and National Opinion Research Center (NORC) (note 18) nationwide estimates are based on random samples and solve the problem of regional bias by their sampling technique, but each represents only one method. Because the two ways of generating estimates for the rates of demoralization in the United States have different strengths and weaknesses, they provide useful material for comparison.

In comparing, first, the estimate of 24.5 percent based on local studies to Dupuy's nationwide study it is heartening to note that his figure of 25.9 percent corresponds so closely to the median of the local studies. In contrast the data from the NORC nationwide study gives a rate of 31.8 percent for demoralization, which is 7.3 percentage points higher than the median of the local studies. However, this difference, which is substantial, may be an artifact of methods.

As we noted earlier, our procedure in determining the rates of demoralization from the 14 local studies involved adopting the authors' cutoff points on the instruments they employed. In these studies the most common cutoff points on the Langner scale were four or more, or seven or more symptoms. Because the figure 31.8 percent from the NORC study is based on the cutoff point of four symptoms, it makes sense that it should be somewhat higher than the 24.5 percent figure based on studies that used both four and seven as cutoff points.

In order to test for the effect of the cutoff point we reanalyzed the data from the NORC study to determine what the result would be with a cutoff of seven, and then compared NORC results based on the cutoff point of four and seven with results from local studies that used one or the other cutoff point on the Langner scale. This comparison is shown in Table 5.4. It is readily apparent that the NORC results correspond quite closely with those from the local studies. The discrepancy in Table 5.3 is apparently a function of cutoff points. However, the problem of differences in results due to the effects of selection of cutoff points remains, since there is no basis for selecting one or the other as correct.

TABLE 5.4

Rates of Demoralization Estimated with Different Cutoff Points on the Langner Scale

Source	Cutoff points	
	4+	7+
Local studies		
Summers et al.	16.6	5.9
Phillips	27.5	8.7
Meile & Haese	32.3	10.9
Yancey et al.	31.8	15.2
Haese & Meile	43.5	18.5
Gaitz & Scott	33.6	14.5
Mueller[a]	43.7	22.5
Median of local studies	32.9	14.8
NORC nationwide study[b]	31.8	13.9

[a]D. Mueller, personal communication.

[b]NORC data were made available by the study director Eleanor Singer, and analyzed by Bruce Link.

Source: Compiled by the authors.

We have dealt with this problem by relying for our estimate on the central tendency of the results from all studies. The consistency found in the data across studies lends confidence to this estimate.

Sex Difference

Women are more likely than men to score as demoralized. In the five local community studies reporting sex differences (Phillips 1966; Phillips and Segal 1969; Edgerton, Bentz, and Hollister 1970; notes 19 and 20) the median rate for women is 32.2 percent demoralized as compared to a median rate of 21.7 percent for men. Within each of the individual studies a higher percentage of women than men scored above the cutoff point. Furthermore, the results of the NORC national sample support the finding of the community studies by showing that the nationwide rate of demoralization for women is 35.5 percent compared to 26.6 percent for men. Similarly, Dupuy's results using the general well being scale show the rate for females to be 30.8 percent and the rate for males to be 20.1 percent. This consistency in results gives us confidence in the finding of a sex difference in rate of demoralization. Although the discrepancy may be due either to differences between men and women in the experience of symptoms of demoralization, or to differences in their willingness to express them, an analysis by Gove and Geerken (1977) suggests that the former is more likely.

Social Class Difference

In the six local community studies that present information on social class (Phillips 1966; Haese and Meile 1967; Edgerton, Bentz, and Hollister 1970; Dohrenwend 1973; notes 21 and 22), the median rate for the lowest social class is 36.4 percent compared to a rate of 9.2 percent for the highest class. Once again, as with the sex difference, the relationship is consistent over all of the studies, that is, each study shows a higher rate for the lowest class than for the highest class. Even more compelling is the fact that each of the studies shows a linear class effect from the lowest class to the highest class such that the highest rate is in the lowest class, the second highest rate in the next class, and so on through the highest class, which has the lowest rate of demoralization.

Again, as with the sex difference, the results of the nationwide NORC and Dupuy studies support the finding from the community

TABLE 5.5

Relation of Percentage of Persons Demoralized to Years of
Education According to NORC and Dupuy Nationwide Studies

	Measure of demoralization			
	Langer 22 item (NORC)		General Well Being (Dupuy)	
	Cutoff point or category identifying demoralized persons			
Years of education	4 +	7+	0–70	0–55
0– 7	49.5	29.3	38.6	16.5
8–11	44.0	21.8	29.6	12.9
12	29.6	11.4		
13–15	20.0	6.3	21.8	6.8
16+	18.4	3.7	17.0	4.7

Source: Compiled by the authors.

studies. Using education as an indicator of social class, Table 5.5
shows the results of these nationwide studies. These consistent results
lend confidence to the observation that there is an inverse relation between social class and rate of demoralization. Again, as with the sex
difference, the analysis by Gove and Geerken (1977) suggests that this
consistent class difference is not an artifact of styles of responding to
interview questions but probably represents a real difference in rates
of demoralization among social classes.

A CROSS-CHECK ON THE ESTIMATE OF THE RATE OF THE
TRUE PREVALENCE OF CLINICAL DISORDER

In Chapter 3 we set forth the hypothesis that the true prevalence of
clinical disorder in the adult population of the United States was
somewhere between 15.9 percent and 25.3 percent. Our estimate in
this regard was based on the central tendencies of a set of studies that
attempted to assess directly the numbers of persons with clinically
significant functional disorders in a variety of settings. Our analysis of
an entirely different set of studies in this section can provide an independent check of this figure.

Returning to Table 5.1 we can calculate the proportion of clinical
cases to screened cases for each of the three studies. For example, in
the Langner study dividing 23.4, the percentage of clinically impaired
people, by 31.2, the percentage screened as "cases," we get .75 or three

clinically impaired individuals to every four who are screened by the 22-item index. Using the proportions derived in this manner from each of the three studies we generated estimates as to the number of clinically impaired persons by multiplying the proportions times 24.5 percent, the estimate derived from 14 studies of the rate of demoralization in the United States. This procedure yields an estimate that 18.4 percent of the population are clinically impaired when we use the proportion from the Langner study, 16.0 percent using the proportion from the Dohrenwend study, and 20.7 percent using the proportion from the Myers and Weissman data. All three of these figures are within the range 15.9–25.3 percent derived from the studies analyzed in Chapter 3 and the average of these three new estimates, 18.4 percent, is close to the midpoint, 20.6, of the previously estimated range. We have then—using a different set of procedures applied to a different set of studies—generated very nearly the same estimate for the rate of clinical disorder in the adult population of the United States.

A QUANTITATIVE NOTE ON THE RELATION OF DEMORALIZATION TO CLINICAL PSYCHIATRIC DISORDER

In interpreting findings concerning rates of clinical disorder and rates of demoralization it is of critical importance to keep in mind that the relationship between the two is an imperfect one. This fact is likely to lead one to ask the question: What proportion of those who are demoralized are also clinically disordered? Drawing once again on the Langner (1962), Dohrenwend (1973), and Myers and Weissman (note 23) studies and using the average percentage of those demoralized who are also clinically impaired, we can estimate that approximately half of the 24.5 percent of the population estimated to be demoralized are also clinically impaired. This result means that in addition to the estimate presented in Chapter 3 that between 15.9 percent and 25.3 percent of the adult population suffer from functional psychiatric disorders, we estimate that another 13 percent are demoralized but not clinically disordered.

SUMMARY AND CONCLUSIONS

The results reported in this chapter suggest that screening scale studies using the Langner 22-item index, HOS, and GWB have been measuring something consistent and meaningful. The stability of results between settings and by sex and social class within studies gives us confidence in this assertion. At the same time, the best evidence available suggests that what is measured by these scales is not "mental illness" or clinical disorder per se but something frequently, but not always, associated with them. Following the work of Jerome Frank (1973) and Dohrenwend et al., (note 24) we have labeled this "something" measured by screening scales "demoralization." Although the particular word chosen to indicate what screening scales measure may be deemed unimportant by some, it is of critical importance that a construct consistent with the evidence be available to lend understanding to the interpretation of past studies and guidance to the implementation of future ones. We feel that the notion of "demoralization" as set forth theoretically by Frank (1973) and supported empirically by the work of Dohrenwend and his colleagues (note 25) is the best current candidate for such a construct. We therefore hypothesize, drawing upon 14 community studies and two nationwide surveys, that

The rate of demoralization in the United States approaches one quarter of the population.

About half of those who are demoralized are also clinically impaired.

The rate of demoralization for women is consistently higher than the rate for men; about 10 percent more women than men are demoralized.

The rate of demoralization is higher in the lowest social class than it is in the highest social class; probably 20–30 percent more of those in the lowest social class are demoralized than in the highest class.

IMPLICATIONS AND RECOMMENDATIONS FOR RESEARCH

One useful way to think about the relationship between rates of demoralization and rates of clinical disorder for research purposes may be to conceptualize four groups: (1) those who are both demoralized and suffer from a clinically significant functional disorder, (2) those who are demoralized only, (3) those who have a clinical disorder but are not demoralized, and (4) those who are neither demoralized nor suffer from a clinically significant disorder. Those in the first group, that is, those who are both demoralized and clinically disordered, can be viewed in terms of Frank's conceptual framework, which posits that demoralization will frequently accompany the experience of a clinically significant disorder. At the same time, however, and still in accordance with Frank's notions, it is possible for persons to become demoralized in the absence of clinical disorder; for example, it is likely that demoralization is a more frequent reaction than clinical psychiatric disorder on the part of previously normal persons facing severe physical illness, or other stressful life events. Such persons would fall into the second group and could be studied and perhaps planned for as a group with special needs. The third group, that is, those who are clinically disordered but not demoralized, might form a particularly interesting group for research purposes. For example, although Frank theorizes that demoralization is likely to occur in conjunction with clinical disorder, it is also possible for persons enjoying favorable conditions of personality resiliency, and material and social supports to be buffered against becoming demoralized. If researchers can isolate such favorable conditions policy makers might be able to institute changes that could relieve some of the suffering associated with psychiatric impairment even in the absence of definitive knowledge of etiology.

APPENDIX

TABLE 5A.1

Fourteen Post 1950 Screening Scale Studies

Study	Number of Respondents	Location	Instrument	Cutoff Point(s)
Manis et al. (1964)	1,183	Kalamazoo, Michigan	Langner	10+
Phillips (1966)	600	State of New Hampshire	Langner	4+
Haese and Meile (1967)	200	City in "plains state"	Langner	7+
Phillips and Segal (1969)	278	Small town New Hampshire	Langner	4+
Meile and Haese (1969)	5,498	Three relatively small communities in "plains state"	Langner	7+
Edgerton et al. (1970)	1,404	Rural North Carolina	HOS	30+
Summers et al. (1971)	1,456	Small town in Illinois	Langner	4+
Gaitz and Scott (1972)	1,141	Houston, Texas	Langner	4+
Yancey et al. (1972)	1,179	Philadelphia, Pa.	Langner	4+
Dohrenwend (1973)	124	Washington Heights, NYC	Langner	4+
Schwab (1973)	315	Rapidly changing county in southeast	Hos	30+
Husaini and Neff [a]	296	Urban and rural sections of Tennessee	HOS	30+
Mueller[b]	363	Sacramento, California	Langner	4+
Warheit[c]	1,636	County in Florida	HOS	30+

[a] B. Husaini and J. Neff, personal communication.
[b] D. Mueller, personal communication.
[c] G. Warheit, personal communication.
Source: Compiled by the authors.

NOTES

1. H. B. M. Murphy, Two stress measures in three cultures—their prognostic efficiency, significance and incongruities. In D. Leigh, J. Noorbakhsh, and C. Izadi (Eds.), International Symposium on Epidemiological Studies in Psychiatry, Tehran, May 20–22, 1974. Available from Dr. H. B. M. Murphy, McGill University, Dept. of Psychiatry, Beatty Hall, 1266 Pine Avenue West, Montreal, P. Q., Canada H3G IA8.

2. H. B. M. Murphy, The meaning of symptom-check scores in mental health surveys: A testing of multiple hypotheses. Unpublished manuscript, April 1977. Available from Dr. Murphy. See note 1.

3. M. Weissman, J. K. Myers, and P. S. Harding, *Psychiatric disorders in a United States urban community: 1975–76.* Unpublished manuscript. Available from Dr. Myrna M. Weissman, Yale University School of Medicine, Department of Psychiatry, 904 Howard Avenue, Suite 2A, New Haven, Connecticut 06519.

4. Murphy, 1974, op. cit.

5. Murphy, 1977, op cit.

6. Weissman, Meyers and Harding, op cit.

7. B. P. Dohrenwend, L. Oksenberg, B. S. Dohrenwend, and D. Cook, *What psychiatric screening scales measure in the general population.* Unpublished manuscript. 1978. Available from Dr. Bruce P. Dohrenwend, Social Psychiatry Research Unit, Tower 3-19H, 100 Haven Avenue, New York, New York 10032.

8. J. Myers, M. Weissman, *Results from a community study in New Haven.* Personal communication. December 1977.

9. Dohrenwend et al., op. cit.

10. Ibid.

11. Meyers and Weissman, op. cit.

12. Dohrenwend et al., op. cit.

13. D. Edwards, R. Yarvis, D. Mueller, H. Zingale, and W. Wagman, *Test-taking and the stability of adjustment scales: Can we assess patient deterioration?* Unpublished manuscript. Available from Dr. Daniel Edwards, Sacramento Medical Center, 4430 U Street, Sacramento, Calif. 95817.

14. D. Mueller, *22-item and general well being.* Results from a community study in Sacramento. Personal communication. November 1977.

15. B. Husaini, and J. Neff, *Preliminary results from a rural Tennessee community.* Personal communication. November 1977.

16. G. Warheit, *Results from a study of a Florida county.* Personal communication. December 1977.

17. Husaini and Neff, op. cit.

18. NORC data were made available by the study director, Eleanor Singer, and analyzed by Bruce Link.

19. Husaini and Neff, op. cit.

20. Warheit, op. cit.

21. Husaini and Neff, op. cit.

22. Warheit, op. cit.

23. Meyers and Weissman, op. cit.

24. Dohrenwend et al., op. cit.

25. Ibid.

REFERENCES

Brodman, K., Erdman, A. J., Lorge, I., Gershensen, C. P., and Wolff, H. G. 1952. The Cornell Medical Index-Health Questionnaire. 3. The evaluation of emotional disturbance. *Journal of Clinical Psychology* 8: 119–124.

Crandell, D. L., and Dohrenwend, B. P. 1967. Some relations among psychiatric symptoms, organic illness, and social class. *American Journal of Psychiatry* 123: 1527–38.

Derogatis, L. R., Lipman, R. S., and Covi, L. 1973. SCL-90: an outpatient psychiatric rating scale—preliminary report. *Psychopharmacology Bulletin* 9: 13–28.

Dohrenwend, B. P. 1966. Social status and psychological disorder: an issue of substance and an issue of method. *American Sociological Review* 31: 14–34.

——. 1973. Some issues in the definition and measurement of psychiatric disorders in general populations. In *Proceedings of the 14th National Meeting of the Public Health Conferences on Records and Statistics* (DHEW Publication No. 74-1214). Washington, D.C.: U.S. Government Printing Office.

Dohrenwend, B. P., and Dohrenwend, B. S. 1969. *Social status and psychological disorder: a causal inquiry.* New York: Wiley.

Dupuy, H. 1974. Utility of the National Center for Health Statistics General Well-Being Schedule in the assessment of self-representations of subjective well-being and distress. *National Conference on Education in Alcohol, Drug Abuse and Mental Health Programs.* Washington, D.C.: DHEW.

Edgerton, J. W., Bentz, W., and Hollister, W. 1970. Demographic factors and responses to stress among rural people. *American Journal of Public Health* 60: 1965–71.

Edwards, D., Yarvis, R., Mueller, D., Zingale, H., and Wagman W. Test-taking and the stability of adjustment scales: can we assess patient deterioration? Unpublished manuscript. Available from Dr. Daniel Edwards, Sacramento Medical Center, 4430 U Street, Sacramento, Calif. 95817.

Frank, J. D. 1973. *Persuasion and Healing.* Baltimore: Johns Hopkins University Press (originally published 1961).

Gaitz, C. M., and Scott, J. 1972. Age and the measurement of mental health. *Journal of Health and Social Behavior* 13: 55–67.

Goldberg, D. P. 1972. *The Detection of Psychiatric Illness by Questionnaire.* London: Oxford University Press.

Gove, W. R., and Geerken, M. R. 1977. Response-bias in surveys of mental health: an empirical investigation. *American Journal of Sociology* 82: 1289–1317.

Gurin, G., Veroff, J., and Feld, S. 1960. *Americans View Their Mental Health.* New York: Basic Books.

Haese, P. N., and Meile, R. L. 1967. The relative effectiveness of two models for scoring the Midtown Psychological Index. *Community Mental Health Journal* 3: 335–42.

Langner, T. S. 1962. A twenty-two item screening score of psychiatric symptoms indicating impairment. *Journal of Health and Human Behavior* 3: 269–76.

Macmillan, A. M. 1957. The health opinion survey: technique for estimating prevalence of psychoneurotic and related types of disorder in communities. *Psychological Reports* 3: 325–9.

Manis, J. G., Brawer, M. J., Hunt, C. L., and Kercher, L. C. 1964. Estimating the prevalence of mental illness. *American Sociological Review* 29: 84–89.

Meile, R. L., and Haese, P. N. 1969. Social status, status incongruence and symptoms of stress. *Journal of Health and Social Behavior* 10: 237–44.

Phillips, D. L. 1966. The "true prevalence" of mental illness in a New England state. *Community Mental Health Journal* 2: 35–40.

Phillips, D. L., and Clancy, K. J. 1969. Some effects of "social desirability" in survey studies. *American Journal of Sociology* 1972, 77: 921–40.

Phillips, D. L., and Segal, B. E. Sexual status and psychiatric illness. *American Sociological Review* 34: 58–72.

Radloff, L. S. 1977. The CES-D Scale: a self-report depression scale for research in the general population. *Applied Psychological Measurement*. 1: 385–401.

Schwab, J. J., McGinnis, N. H., and Warheit, G. J. 1973. Social psychiatric impairment: racial comparisons. *American Journal of Psychiatry* 130: 183–7.

Seiler, L. H. 1973. The 22-item scale used in field studies of mental illness: a question of method, a question of substance, and a question of theory. *Journal of Health and Social Behavior* 14: 252–64.

Star, S. A. 1950a. The screening of psychoneurotics in the army: technical development of tests. In S. A. Stouffer, L. Guttman, E. A. Suchman, P. F. Lazarsfeld, S. A. Star, and J. A. Clausen (Eds.), *Measurement and Prediction*. Princeton, N.J.: Princeton University Press, 486–547.

———. 1950b. The screening of psychoneurotics: comparison of psychiatric diagnoses and test scores at all induction stations. In S. A. Stouffer, L. Guttman, E. A. Suchman, P. F. Lazarsfeld, S. A. Star, and J. A. Clausen (Eds.), *Measurement and Prediction*. Princeton, N.J.: Princeton University Press, 438–567.

Summers, G. F., Seiler, L. H., and Hough, R. L. 1971. Psychiatric symptoms: cross validation with a rural sample. *Rural Sociology* 36: 367–78.

Tousignant, M. G. D., and Lachapelle, R. 1974. Some considerations concerning the validity and use of the health opinion survey. *Journal of Health and Social Behavior* 15: 241–52.

Weissman, M., Sholomskas, D., Dottenjer, M., Prusoff, B., and Locke, B. 1977. Assessing depressive symptoms in five psychiatric populations: a validation study. *American Journal of Epidemiology* 106: 203–14.

Yancey, W. L., Rigsby, L., and McCarthy, J. D. 1972. Social position and self-evaluation: the relative importance of race. *American Journal of Sociology* 78: 338–59.

6

FORMULATION OF HYPOTHESES ABOUT THE RATIO OF UNTREATED TO TREATED CASES IN THE TRUE PREVALENCE STUDIES OF FUNCTIONAL PSYCHIATRIC DISORDERS IN ADULTS IN THE UNITED STATES

Bruce Link
Bruce P. Dohrenwend

In 1855, Edward Jarvis, a New England physician and epidemiologist, submitted a report to the Governor and Council of Massachusetts on what is probably the most complete and influential attempt to investigate the true prevalence of psychiatric disorder conducted in the nineteenth century (Jarvis 1971). Jarvis' effort to count untreated as well as treated cases of "insanity" was undertaken because he was well aware of the inadequacy of information based on treated rates to reveal either the magnitude of problems of insanity or the nature of its distribution in the population. He had, in fact, conducted a classic study of how admission rates varied with geographic distance from the mental hospital (Jarvis 1866).

There have been dramatic illustrations that the problem is an important one. For example, Eaton and Weil (1955) would have confirmed the hypothesis that the Hutterites were a utopia of mental health if they had used hospital admissions to measure the rates of psychiatric disorder. There were no Hutterites in mental hospitals at the time these investigators did their research. Yet, as Eaton and Weil found on the basis of key informant reports and interviews with members of the Hutterite communities, this was definitely not a society that immunized its members against the development of psychiatric disorders. Furthermore, if Srole et al. (1962) had relied solely on admission to treatment with members of the mental health professions to define a case, they would have concluded that overall rates of psychiatric disorder were highest in the higher social classes in the section of Manhattan in New York City that they studied. The opposite proved to be the case when they based their estimates of the number of cases on psychiatric symptoms reported in interviews with a representative sample of the general population in that area.

Despite its importance, surprisingly little has been written on the relation of untreated to treated rates of psychiatric disorder in the general population. Part of the problem is that it is difficult to get unduplicated records of persons who have received psychiatric treatment in diverse places and diverse settings. Moreover, only a minority of true prevalence studies reported which of the subjects judged to be cases had ever been in treatment with members of the mental health professions.

So far, we have found 13 epidemiologic studies, including Jarvis' 1855 investigation and one study using a screening scale (Phillips 1966), from which cases never in treatment could be separated from cases ever in treatment with members of the mental health professions. Most of the U.S. studies provided data on persons in treatment who suffered from any type of disorder and did not break their figures down according to types of disorder. However, some studies present the opposite problem; data were provided for particular types of disorder but not for overall rates. Table 6.1 presents our tabulations from all of these studies.

OVERALL PERCENTAGE OF TRUE CASES TO HAVE HAD TREATMENT

The overall median proportion of true cases in treatment for the 11 studies providing the necessary information is 26.7 percent. It appears, then, that only about 25 percent of those found to be suffering from a clinically significant disorder had ever been in treatment. Although we cannot have a great deal of confidence in this figure, given the diversity in the studies, we can say that it may underestimate the number of true cases who had not received treatment. Our reasoning is, first, that three of the five studies (Rosanoff 1917; Roth 1942; Jarvis 1971) that found higher proportions of true cases in treatment were conducted before 1950 and used much narrower criteria for identifying a case than are used today. Furthermore, each of these three studies relied heavily on key informant rather than more intensive case finding techniques. As a result only the most severe, visible, and socially disruptive persons were identified as cases. The relatively high proportion of true cases in treatment reported in these studies is probably due to this constriction in the range of individuals included as cases.

Second, the study that provides the median figure of 26.7 percent is the investigation by Srole et al. (1962) conducted in midtown Manhattan. As Jarvis (1866) pointed out in the nineteenth century, and as Srole and his colleagues emphasized more recently (1962, pp. 129–132), the availability of services determines, in large part, the number of persons who will seek treatment in a given area. Srole and his colleagues took note of the fact that New York City, and Manhattan in particular, probably has the most highly developed system of psychiatric care in the country. Since the median figure of 26.7 percent comes from this setting, it may overestimate the number of true cases receiving treatment in the country as a whole.

Let us adopt the conservative figure of 26.7 percent as representing the proportion of true cases ever in treatment. Using the estimate, presented in Chapter 3, that 16–25 percent of the population suffer from a clinical disorder, we can now calculate that between 12 and 18 percent of the U.S. population is suffering from a clinically significant disorder and has never received treatment for it from a mental health professional. Even allowing for a possible 3 percent who are receiving treatment solely from general practitioners (Locke and Gardner 1969), this conservatively estimated number of untreated cases is staggering. Moreover, there may well be substantial numbers of persons who do not have clinically significant disorders who are in treatment with members of the mental health professions. The National Opinion Research Center (NORC) study showed that 21.9 percent of those currently suffering from the kind of psychological distress that we have construed as demoralization, here measured by the Langner screening scale, said that they had been in treatment for an emotional problem.[1] It is unlikely, given the relation described in the last chapter between such measures of distress and clinical disorder, that all of these distressed persons are suffering from clinical psychiatric disorders. An important question for future research, therefore, is to establish not only what proportion of true clinical cases remain untreated, but also what proportion of those in treatment are not suffering from clinical psychiatric disorders. Still more important is the question: What difference does it make?

PSYCHOSIS AND SCHIZOPHRENIA

The median proportion of true cases ever in treatment for those suffering from psychotic disorders is 59.7 percent based on evidence from seven studies, and the corresponding rate for schizophrenia is 83.3 percent based on six studies. If these figures are accurate they mean that two out of every five persons with psychosis and one out of every five

TABLE 6.1

Relation of True to Treated Rates

Study	Sample or Population N	True Rate (%)	Treated Rate (%)	N of True Cases	Percent True Cases Treated
Overall					
Roth (1943)	26,100	.4[a]	.21	104	52.0
Jarvis (1971)	1,124,676	.234	.12	2,632	51.2
Rosanoff (1917)	83,960	1.9	.79	663	41.6
Myers and Weissman[b]	511	15.1 (definite)		77 (definite and probable)	40.0
		2.7 (probable)			
Cole (1957)	350	31.7	12.3	111	38.7
Srole et al. (1962)	1,660	23.4	13.4	389	26.7
Brunetti (1973)	683	5.7	1.3	39	23.0
NORC[c]	1,318	31.8	14.0	419	22.0
Phillips (1966)	599	27.5	14.2	165	21.8
Dohrenwend (1970)	257	27.6	9.7	71	19.7
Hare and Shaw (1965)	1,940	20.7	3.0	404	8.5
Warheit[d]	1,636	28.2		461	7.8

Study					
Hagnell (1966)	2,283	15.6	5.4		
Helgason (1964)	5,395	28.6	4.6		
Psychosis					
Strömgren (1950)	45,000	1.20	1.00		85.3
Cohen and Fairbank (1938)	40,565	.83	.67	335	81.5
Lemkau (1942)	55,100	.67	.53	367	80.1
Helgason (1964)	5,395	5.1	3.00	273	59.7
Bremer (1951)	1,604	2.9	1.30	38	55.3
Brugger (1931)					55.1
Brunetti (1973)	683	1.2	.59	8	50.0
Schizophrenia					
Bremer (1951)	1,080	.56	.56	6	100.0
Cohen and Fairbank (1938)	40,565	.31	.30	127	96.1
Essen-Möller (1956)	2,520	.67	.59	17	88.2
Helgason (1964)	5,395	.67	.56	36	83.3
Böök (1953)	8,981	.95	.75	85	78.8
Eaton and Weil (1955)	8,542	.11	.06	9	55.6
Brunetti (1973)	683	.59	.29	4	50.0

[a] Cases judged eligible for hospital.
[b] J. Myers and M. Weissman, personal communication.
[c] NORC data were made available by the study director, Eleanor Singer, and analyzed by Bruce Link.
[d] G. Warheit, personal communication.
Source: Compiled by the authors.

with schizophrenia have never received treatment from a mental health professional. Sizable proportions of persons with severe problems are in the community and untreated.

With regard to schizophrenia and perhaps the psychotic disorders as a whole the problem may be even more substantial than these figures suggest. Consider in this regard the relationship between severity of disorder and the rate of true cases in treatment demonstrated by the medians of 26.7 percent for overall disorder, 59.7 for the psychoses, and the 83.3 percent for schizophrenia. The more severe the disorder the more likely a person is to have been in treatment. This relationship coincides so neatly with the common sense expectation that the more ill a person is the more likely he or she is to enter treatment that it might divert our attention from examining other reasons for the relationship. One possibility is that the diagnosticians in many of the true prevalence studies were reluctant to label individuals "manic depressive" or "schizophrenic" in the absence of a treatment history and corroborating evidence from treatment records. An epidemiologic study by Helgason (1964) suggests that this may have happened. He reported two levels of diagnostic certainty, those considered definite cases of a particular clinical entity and those of a more questionable nature. He then reported how many of each level of certainty had been in treatment. For schizophrenia 83.3 percent (30/36) had been in treatment whereas only 33 percent (2/6) of the questionable cases had received care. Similarly, for manic depressive psychosis the figures were 65.4 percent (53/81) and 36.4 percent (8/22) respectively. It seems, then, that diagnoses of severe disorders were made much more reluctantly in the absence of treatment history. If this diagnostic bias is widespread in epidemiologic studies, then the median figure for the percentage of true cases in treatment for schizophrenia, and perhaps for the psychoses as a whole, may be too high an estimate. There may be even more persons with untreated psychotic disorders than our figures suggest.

TREATED VERSUS TRUE RATES BY THE DEMOGRAPHIC CHARACTERISTICS OF THE RESPONDENTS

Most of the evidence on the relation between true and treated rates reported thus far was gleaned from the true prevalence studies. Unfortunately very few of these studies reported their results in a manner that allows the reader to compare true to treated rates by demographic variables. The material that follows is from several relatively recent U.S. studies, and reports true versus treated rates by sex (four studies), age (three studies), social class (three studies), marital status (three studies), and urban–rural location (three studies). Despite the paucity of studies and the preponderance among them of those using screening scales, this evidence can help us answer two questions. First, it can tell us whether treated rates show the same pattern of relations with demographic variables as true rates of clinical disorder and/or severe demoralization and thus can help us decide whether treated rates can be substituted, at least for some purposes, for true rates as epidemiologic measures. Second, by determining the proportion of true cases who receive treatment in various demographic categories we can get some idea of what segments of the distressed or disordered population are receiving the most and what segments the least amount of treatment.

The three studies used consistently in the following tables were conducted by Myers and Weissman, Warheit and NORC.[2-4] The Myers and Weissman study was conducted in an urban setting, New Haven, Connecticut, and was a third stage follow-up of a sample interviewed in 1967 and 1969. The method of assessment of true cases in this study was based on the Research Diagnostic Criteria (see Chapter 3) and thus reflects an assessment of the true prevalence of clinical disorder. The Warheit study conducted in Florida contains both rural and urban settings and used the Health Opinion Survey (HOS), a screening scale, to assess its true cases. The NORC study used the Langner 22-item screening scale, similar to the HOS, to assess the true prevalence of distress in a national sample. The tables that follow use these three studies to show (1) the "true" rate versus the treated rate and (2) the proportion of true cases ever to have been in treatment with a mental health professional by several demographic variables.

Table 6.2 shows true versus treated rates by sex. Each of the studies shows females to have a higher treated rate and a higher true rate than males. In addition, one of the four, the NORC study, showed that treatment was sought by substantially more females than males among those who were classified as true cases.

Table 6.3 shows urban and rural comparisons from the NORC and Warheit studies. In the NORC study, the highest treated rate was found in the suburban areas and the lowest true rate in this setting. This finding indicates that for the study of rural–urban differences the two rates are not interchangeable. Table 6.3 also shows that urban people who experienced distress were more likely to have received treatment than similar rural people in both studies.

Table 6.4 shows that both the true rate and the treated rate are higher for persons who have been divorced or separated than for married persons. It also indicates that among persons identified as cases

TABLE 6.2

Relation of True to Treated Rates by Sex

Study (instrument)	Sex	N	True Rate (%)	Treated Rate (%)	N of True Cases	Percent True Cases Treated
Myers and Weissman (RDC)	Male	228	32.6[a] (16.1)	13.3	71	36.6
	Female	291	47.8[a] (18.9)	18.2	139	35.9
Warheit (HOS)	Male	733	21.7	b	159	7.5
	Female	903	33.4	b	302	7.9
NORC (Langner)	Male	546	26.6	11.3	145	15.9
	Female	772	35.5	15.9	274	25.2
Phillips (Langner)	Male	296	20.6	13.5	61	19.7
	Female	303	34.3	14.9	104	23.1

[a]First figure refers to lifetime diagnosis, that is, whether the person ever had a disorder, and figure in parentheses refers to current diagnosis.
[b]Data not available: Number of people who are not true cases but who have been in treatment is not known.
Source: Compiled by the authors.

TABLE 6.3

Relation of True to Treated Rates by Urban–Rural Study Site

Study (instrument)	Study Site	N	True Rate (%)	Treated Rate (%)	N of True Cases	Percent True Cases Treated
Warheit (HOS)	Rural	507	33.3	*	169	5.3
	Urban	1,125	25.9	*	291	9.3
NORC (Langner)	Rural	435	32.9	11.0	143	18.9
	Suburban	375	27.5	16.3	103	26.2
	Urban	365	32.1	15.6	117	23.1

*Data not available: Number of people who are not true cases but who have been in treatment is not known.
Source: Compiled by the authors.

TABLE 6.4

Relation of True to Treated Rates by Marital Status

Study (Instrument)	Marital Status	N	True Rate (%)	Treated Rate (%)	N of True Cases	Percent True Cases Treated
Myers and Weissman (RDC)	Married	375	38.7* (16.3)	15.2	145	35.2
	Single	22	50.0* (22.7)	36.4	11	72.8
	Separated/ divorced	43	67.4* (20.9)	30.2	29	44.8
	Widowed	69	36.2* (21.7)	5.8	25	16.0
NORC (Langner)	Married	841	28.9	12.7	243	21.4
	Single	171	33.9	14.0	58	22.4
	Separated	43	60.5	30.2	26	23.1
	Divorced	96	40.6	32.3	39	41.0
	Widowed	167	31.7	6.0	53	9.4

*First figure refers to lifetime diagnosis, that is, whether the person ever had a disorder, and figure in parentheses refers to current diagnosis.

Source: Compiled by the authors.

of psychological disorder or severe distress in the community, those who are divorced or separated are more likely to have been in treatment than those who are currently married. Somewhat surprisingly, the widowed who were identified as cases were the least likely to have been in treatment. This finding may, however, be related to the fact that the widowed are probably older, on the average, than other marital status groups, together with the age difference in proportion who have been in treatment, which is shown in Table 6.5.

As this table shows, the proportion of true cases who have been in treatment declines sharply with age. These figures, it should be recalled, refer to the number of persons ever in treatment. Given the same propensity to seek treatment, and roughly equal true rates across age groups, we would expect older persons to have higher rather than lower treated rates since they have had a longer period at risk of being in treatment. Thus, the age difference implies an even larger increase in lifetime rates of treatment between generations, a matter that we will return to shortly.

Note that, unlike the treated rates, the true rates reported by these studies do not show a consistent decline with age. This difference in relation to age again indicates that true and treated rates are not interchangeable.

Table 6.5 also shows that young people considered true cases are more likely than older people to have been in treatment. This finding nicely complements the results from a recent replication of a study, published in *Americans View Their Mental Health* (1960), of a national sample in 1957. Comparing results from a similar sample studied in 1976, Kulka, Veroff, and Douvan found that whereas in the earlier study 14 percent had reported having gone to a mental health professional for help, in the later study nearly twice this proportion, 26 percent, reported seeking such help.[5] This change over time and the greater propensity of younger people to seek help may be two reflections of the same underlying social trend. We should note further that these results imply that figures concerning proportions of "true" cases who receive treatment derived from past studies may be lower than figures that would be obtained if a study were done today. This change may compensate for other factors, previously described, that led us to speculate that the figures for number of untreated cases that we have extracted from available studies are conservative.

Table 6.6 is striking in that it shows two relationships that are each quite consistent across studies and are contrary to each other. The first is an inverse relation between class and the true rate of psychological disorder. The second is a direct relation between class and treated rates. Clearly, in studies of social class and mental illness treated rates will lead to different conclusions than true rates. A further implication

TABLE 6.5

Relation of True to Treated Rates by Age

Study (instrument)	Age	N	True Rate (%)	Treated Rate (%)	N of True Cases	Percent True Cases Treated
Myers and Weissman (RDC)	26–35	109	50.5[a] (18.3)	25.7	55	45.4
	36–45	101	44.6[a] (16.8)	20.8	45	40.0
	46–55	100	46.0[a] (20.0)	16.0	46	34.8
	56–65	89	38.2[a] (22.5)	10.1	34	26.7
	66+	110	27.3[a] (11.8)	7.3	30	26.7

Warheit (HOS)	16–22	269	25.3	[b]	68	20.6
	23–29	311	16.1	[b]	50	10.0
	30–44	410	23.9	[b]	98	10.2
	45–59	330	34.8	[b]	115	4.3
	60+	314	41.1	[b]	129	1.6
NORC (Langner)	Up to 21	95	33.7	11.6	32	25.0
	22–30	315	31.7	19.4	100	27.0
	31–40	245	31.4	18.8	77	26.0
	41–50	181	30.4	16.0	55	29.1
	51–60	206	29.6	10.7	61	16.4
	61–70	146	31.5	5.5	46	10.9
	70+	125	37.7	5.6	47	12.8

[a]First figure refers to lifetime diagnosis, that is, whether the person ever had a disorder, and figure in parentheses refers to current diagnosis.

[b]Data not available: Number of people who are not true cases but who have been in treatment is not known.

Source: Compiled by the authors.

145

TABLE 6.6

Relation of True to Treated Rates by Class

Study (instrument)	Class	N	True Rate (%)	Treated Rate (%)	N of True Cases	Percent True Cases Treated
Myers and Weissman (RDC)	Low-V	121	42.2[a] (22.3)	14.0	51	31.3
	IV	225	40.4[a] (17.8)	15.5	91	37.4
	I+II+III	164	41.5[a] (14.0)	18.3	68	39.4
Warheit (HOS)	Low	215	54.5	b	117	2.6
	2	378	36.5	b	138	8.7
	3	479	24.6	b	118	8.5
	4	341	16.7	b	57	12.3
	High	223	13.9	b	31	12.9
NORC (Langner)	Low	188	49.5	9.6	93	15.1
	2	225	44.0	15.9	99	28.3
	3	507	29.6	10.8	150	19.3
	4	205	20.0	14.6	41	24.4
	High	190	18.4	23.7	35	28.6

[a]First figure refers to lifetime diagnosis, that is, whether the person ever had a disorder, and figure in parentheses refers to current diagnosis.

[b]Data not available; number of people who are not true cases but who have been in treatment is not known.

Source: Compiled by the authors.

of this difference is, as Table 6.6 shows, that those deemed true cases are much more likely to receive treatment if they are from a higher class. Thus, although it is the poor, according to evidence presented here and in the third chapter, who are most likely to be in need, it is the relatively wealthy who are most likely to receive care.

We should note that this conclusion does not appear to be affected by the results reported by Kulka and his colleagues showing increased use by Americans of mental health professionals between 1957 and 1976.[6] Although the proportionate increase is greater in lower than higher classes, a direct relationship between social class and percentage treated by a mental health professional was found in the later as well as the earlier study.

SUMMARY OF FINDINGS

Our exploration of the relationship between true and treated rates of psychological disorder in the true prevalence studies has led us to the following findings:

Large proportions, perhaps 75 percent, of individuals suffering from either a clinical psychological disorder or a significant degree of psychological distress have never been in treatment.

For the more severe psychotic disorders large proportions, perhaps as many as 45 percent of the cases, have never received treatment from a mental health professional.

Even for schizophrenia it seems that a large minority, perhaps 20 percent, have never been in contact with a mental health professional.

There is a tendency for women, given an equal level of distress, to seek treatment more frequently than men.

People living in urban areas are more likely to receive treatment than people in rural areas.

Separated and divorced persons are more likely to seek treatment, given an equal level of distress, than are married persons or widows.

Younger persons suffering from distress are more likely than older persons to have been in treatment.

While persons in the lower social classes are more likely to suffer from psychological distress they are less likely to have been in treatment with a mental health professional.

CONCLUSIONS

The evidence strongly suggests that true rates cannot be used interchangeably with treated rates. The sociodemographic variables of age, urban–rural location, and class show consistently different patterns of relations with psychological disorder depending on which rate is chosen. For sex and marital status, although the relation to psychological disorder is in the same direction for true and treated rates, it is not of the same magnitude. Thus, even for these variables treated and true rates should not be considered interchangeable.

It should be clear that this evidence does not mean that one measure is intrinsically superior to the other. Each measure has meaning and provides important information. Instead the evidence indicates that the two rates do not measure the same thing and that it would be unwise to consider them to do so.

An important question raised but not sufficiently answered here is, What is the difference between the two rates, that is, what is different about a typical "true" case as opposed to a typical treated case that makes the two rates differ. This issue, touched upon here, remains an important one for further research.

NOTES

1. NORC data were made available by the study director, Eleanor Singer, and analyzed by Bruce Link.

2. J. Myers, and M. Weissman, *Results from a community study in New Haven*. Personal communication. December 1977.

3. G. Warheit, *Results from a study of a Florida county*. Personal communication. December 1977.

4. NORC, op. cit.

5. R. A. Kulka, J. Veroff, and E. Douvan, Social class and the use of professional help for personal problems: 1957 and 1976. Unpublished manuscript.

6. Ibid.

REFERENCES

Babigian, H. M. 1975. Schizophrenia: epidemiology. In A. M. Freedman, H. I. Kaplan, B. J. Sadock (Eds.), *Comprehensive Textbook of Psychiatry*. II. Baltimore: William and Wilkins.

Böök, J. A. 1953. A genetic and neuropsychiatric investigation of a north Swedish population, with special regard to schizophrenia and mental deficiency. *Acta Genetica et Statistica Medica* 4: 1–100.

Bremer, J. 1951. A social psychiatric investigation of a small community in northern Norway. *Acta Psychiatrica et Neurologica Scandinavica*, suppl. 62.

Brugger, C. 1931. Versuch einer Geisteskrankanzählung in Thüringen. *Zeitschrift für die gesamte Neurologie und Psychiatrie* 133: 352–90.

Brunetti, P. M. 1973. Prevalence des troubles mentaux dans une population rurale du Vaucluse: donnée nouvelles et recapitulatives. *L'Hygiene Mentale* 1.

Cohen, B. M., and Fairbank, R. 1938. Statistical contributions from the mental hygiene study of the Eastern Health District of Baltimore. II. Psychosis in the Eastern Health District in 1933. *American Journal of Psychiatry* 94: 1377–95.

Cole, N. J., Branch, C. H. H., and Orla, M. 1957. Mental illness. *AMA Archives of Neurology and Psychiatry* 77: 393–8.

Dohrenwend, B. 1970. Psychiatric disorder in general populations: problems of the untreated case. *American Journal of Public Health* 60: 1052–64.

Eaton, J. W., and Weil, R. J. 1955. *Culture and Mental Disorders*. Glencoe, Ill.: Free Press.

Essen-Möller, E. 1956. Individual traits and morbidity in a Swedish rural population, *Acta Psychiatrica et Neurologica Scandinavica*, suppl. 100.

Hagnell, O. 1966. *A Prospective Study of the Incidence of Mental Disorder*. Stockholm: Svenska Bokförlaget Norstedts–Bonniers.

Hare, E. H., and Shaw, G. K. 1965. *Mental Health on a New Housing Estate*. New York: Oxford University Press.

Helgason, T. 1964. Epidemiology of mental disorders in Iceland. *Acta Psychiatrica Scandinavica*, suppl. 173.

Jarvis, E. 1866. Influence of distance from and nearness to an insane hospital on its use by the people. *American Journal of Psychiatry* 22: 361–406.

————. 1971. *Insanity and Idiocy in Massachusetts*, Cambridge, Mass.: Harvard University Press.

Lemkau, P., Tietze, C., and Cooper. M. 1942. Mental hygiene problems in an urban district. *Mental Hygiene*, 26: 100–19.

Locke, B. Z., and Gardner, E. A. 1969. Psychiatric disorders among the patients of general practitioners and internists. *Public Health Reports* 84: 167–73.

Phillips, D. C. 1966. The "true prevalence" of mental illness in a New England state. *Community Mental Health Journal* 2: 35–40.

Rosanoff, H. J. 1917. Survey of mental disorders in Nassau County, New York, July–October 1916. *Psychiatric Bulletin* 2: 109–231.

Roth, W. F., and Luton, F. B. 1943. The mental hygiene program in Tennessee. *American Journal of Psychiatry* 99: 662–75.

Srole, L., Langner, T. S., Michael, S. T., Opler, M. K., and Rennie, T. A. C. 1962. *Mental Health in the Metropolis*. New York: McGraw-Hill.

Strömgren, E. 1950. Statistical and population studies within psychiatry: methods and principal results. In *Actualites Scientifiques et Industrielles, Congress Internationale de Psychiatrie*. 6. Psychiatric Society 155–88. Paris: Herman and Cie.

7
SUMMARY AND CONCLUSIONS

Bruce P. Dohrenwend

In Chapter 1, we point out that we decided to cast the results of our analyses in the form of hypotheses rather than in the form of firm conclusions because of the serious methodological problems apparent in the relevant epidemiological investigations. We indicated, however, that the results of our analyses proved considerably firmer than we had anticipated. In this concluding chapter we summarize the best hypotheses we have developed about the magnitude and distribution of problems of mental health in the U.S. population, and we will say something more about the firmness of the evidence on which these hypotheses are based.

MAGNITUDE OF PROBLEMS OF MENTAL HEALTH AND THEIR DISTRIBUTION IN THE POPULATION

The term "prevalence" in the following summary refers to the number of cases found in existence during a brief study period somewhere between a point in time and a year. Consider first the main results for children on the basis of the evidence available, we hypothesize as follows:

That the true prevalence of clinical maladaptation among school children in a representative sample of U.S. communities is unlikely to average less than 12 percent and is likely to vary according to age, social class, ethnic group, and geographic region. Studies providing the relevant information indicate that the large majority of these maladjusted children were not receiving treatment.

150

We hypothesize that in a representative sample of U.S. communities, the true prevalence of psychiatric disorders with no known organic basis for adults below age 60–65 would be:

—An overall rate for the aggregated functional disorders of between 16 and 25 percent.
—Between 0.6 and 3.0 percent for schizophrenia.
—About 0.3 percent for affective psychosis.
—Between 8.0 and 15.0 percent for neurosis.
—About 7.0 percent for personality disorder.

For the elderly over age 60, we hypothesize on the basis of available evidence that rates of psychiatric disorders are as follows:

—An aggregated overall rate of functional and organic psychiatric disorders of 18.0 to 24.5 percent.
—Organic psychoses, 3.5 to 5.5 percent.
—Functional psychoses, 3.5 percent.
—Neuroses, 6.0 to 10.5 percent.
—Personality disorders, 5.0 percent.

In addition to clinical cases of psychiatric disorder, we hypothesize that

—About 13 percent of the population on the average in a representative sample of U.S. communities would show severe psychological and somatic distress that was not accompanied by clinical psychiatric disorder.

Whether accompanied by diagnosable psychiatric disorder as it is in some persons, or without the presence of such disorder as in others, we think that Frank's concept of "demoralization" is the best description of this type of distress (*Persuasion and Healing* 1973).

—Considering all demoralized persons, those with and those without psychiatric disorders, we estimate the rate of demoralization at about 25 percent at any given time.

As with children, there are likely to be sharp differences in rates of psychiatric disorders among adults from different social backgrounds. On the basis of the evidence, we hypothesize that if a representative sample of U.S. communities were studied, sharp differences would be found in rates of various types of disorders for males by contrast with females, and for higher versus lower social classes.

—Rates of neurosis and of affective psychosis are likely to be consistently higher among women.
—Rates of personality disorder are likely to be consistently higher among men.
—Rates of overall functional psychiatric disorder, and the subtypes, schizophrenia and personality disorder, are likely to be consistently highest in the lowest social class.
—Rates of demoralization are likely to be consistently higher in women than in men and consistently higher in lower than in higher social classes.

With regard to the treatment of identified cases among adults in the general population we hypothesize that

Only about a quarter of those with clinically significant functional disorders have ever received treatment from mental health professionals.
Even for the most severe disorders such as schizophrenia and other psychoses, large minorities, perhaps 20% for schizophrenia and 40% for all psychoses, have never received treatment from mental health professionals.

HOW FIRM IS THE EVIDENCE?

The evidence for these hypotheses proved firmer and more persuasive than we had anticipated. The reason is that not only did the consistencies in relationships between important demographic variables and various types of disorders that we and others had discovered in previous analyses tend to hold up in this most recent assessment, but also it was possible for the first time for us to compare and check against each other various differing approaches to assessing the magnitude of problems of mental health. Recall some examples of these cross-checks.

First, in the analyses of studies of clinical maladaptation in childhood it was possible to extrapolate from findings from British methodological studies of relations between teacher ratings and parent ratings to the results that would be achieved in substantive studies using one or the other procedure. The actual results of the U.S. studies made sense in terms of these extrapolations.

Second, one of the bodies of literature that we dealt with defined cases in terms of judgments by psychiatrists whereas another used objective test items calibrated against patient criterion groups to screen for cases. Fortunately, there were at least three studies that provided a comparison of the two procedures for identifying cases. It was thus possible to estimate what proportion of actual cases would be screened by the screening scales and check whether these results agreed with the findings from the studies using clinical judgments. They did.

We believe that psychiatric screening scales actually measure a demoralization syndrome—a constellation of symptoms of psychological and somatic distress that is only weakly and often only indirectly related to the clinical psychiatric disorders described in psychiatric nomenclatures. We have argued nevertheless that demoralization is important in its own right.

One of the problems in investigating rates of demoralization in the United States was that most studies focused on one or another community rather than the U.S. population as a whole. Moreover, the communities were not picked to be representative of all U.S. communities. Nevertheless, to recall our third major example of successful crosschecks, it was possible to compare the results of two nationwide studies with the findings from the community studies. The results of the nationwide studies and the aggregated community studies proved to be remarkably similar, thereby enhancing our confidence in the representativeness of the community study findings and the accuracy of the two nationwide investigations.

IMPLICATIONS OF THE RESULTS

It is only recently that a sufficient number of epidemiologic studies of general populations have accumulated to permit analyses leading to more sensible and less arbitrary statements about the scope of the problems of mental illness than have been made in the past. Some of the most important implications of the analyses stem from the estimates they yield of the sheer size of the rates of untreated cases by contrast with the rates of treated cases. Only minorities of those judged to be cases in epidemiologic studies actually get into treatment with members of the mental health professions. It would seem that there is a kind of screen of public attitudes and reactions that sorts and sifts individuals showing deviant behavior. In the sorting process, only small proportions of those judged to be psychiatric cases in epidemiologic studies are actually channeled into treatment by members of the mental health professions.

Hollingshead and Redlich (1958) termed the attitudes and reactions that form the basis of the sorting process "lay appraisals" and pointed out that they formed the public counterpart of clinical diagnosis by psychiatrists. To date, we know very little about how these screens of lay appraisals operate in general populations despite the fact that we know quite a lot about public attitudes (Rabkin 1975), the utilization of mental health services (Greenley and Mechanic 1976; Kramer 1976; Regier, Goldberg, and Taube 1978; Tischler et al. 1975), and the groups at highest risk for various types of psychiatric disorder (see, for example, preceding chapters of this book). The reason is that studies of public attitudes towards mental illness and studies of actual use of mental health services have not been combined with studies of the true prevalence and true incidence of psychiatric disorders in general populations and their fluctuations over time with changes in treatment modalities. Thus, we simply do not know to what extent the screen of lay appraisal processes works at cross-purposes with goals of delivering services as efficiently and effectively as possible to the persons and groups in greatest need. It is difficult to see how rational plans for the delivery of mental health services can be made and evaluated until such research is undertaken on a continuing basis.

The charge from the President's Commission to the Task Panel on the Scope of the Problem did not ask only for information on the scope of problems of mental illness in relation to the allocation of services, research, and manpower "to ease the burden in future years." The charge was also to make recommendations about prevention based on knowledge of the antecedents of disorders and knowledge of vulnerability and risk—in sum, on the basis of knowledge of etiology.

The fact of the matter is, however, that epidemiologic studies have provided clues to causation and posed issues and questions rather than firm conclusions. For example, we know a great deal about how different types of psychiatric disorder are distributed in the population according to sex and social class. This information raises important issues for further research on etiology—for example, on the part played by biology in contrast to social role in explaining why males have higher rates of the acting out types of personality disorder while women have higher rates of neurosis; or on the classic social stress–social selection question of whether rates of some types of disorder such as schizophrenia are highest in the lowest social class because of the stressful environments lower class individuals experience or because persons with such disorders are selected into the lowest social class due to inability to function at higher levels. It has not, however, provided firm facts about causation or the precise estimates of risk that are needed as a basis for preventive action. Nor has it provided a set of widely accepted case identification and classification procedures for further research.

THE FUTURE

The body of epidemiologic studies that we reviewed provided far less information than was called for by the charge from the president's commission. We think, however, that it provided far more than anyone, including ourselves, had any right to expect. For the most part, the value of these studies in psychiatric epidemiology does not reside in a small minority of particular investigations that stand out above all those that have accumulated over the past 25–30 years. Rather, it lies in trends and consistencies across the total number of relevant epidemiologic studies of children, young and middle-aged adults, and the older persons that we could discover. The primitive methods used to conduct these studies have meant that little reliance can be placed on one or two individual investigations, and it is doubtful that further accumulations of similar studies will provide much additional knowledge.

What is needed are far better methods for future studies that will not only test previous estimates of rates for particular types of disorder and their distribution according to demographic variables, but that will also break new ground. Fortunately, newer approaches to measurement and classification of psychopathology now in developmental stages are beginning to reflect important advances in biological and behavioral research in this field. For example, the work on a new edition of the American Psychiatric Association's Diagnostic and Statistical Manual is being undertaken with recognition of the need for objective and reliable procedures for combining data on signs, symptoms, and functioning into diagnostic syndromes (Task Force on Nomenclature and Statistics of the American Psychiatric Association 1978). In England a computer program has been developed to perform this task with reference to the psychiatric section of the International Classification of Diseases (Wing, Cooper, and Sartorius 1974). New interview instruments of various types have been developed with the aim of providing reliable and valid data on signs and symptoms for such classification systems (for example, Dohrenwend et al.[1]; Endicott and Spitzer 1978; Wing, Cooper, and Sartorius 1974). If such developments are suitably nourished, it should very soon be within our research capability to provide reliable comparative data on the incidence and duration of mental disorders as well as their current or point prevalence in general populations, on patterns of utilization of service facilities by persons with different types of mental disorder, on evaluation of outcomes of different therapies, and on the effectiveness of preventive efforts. In addition, such advances in methods should permit basic research on the etiologic issues.

Care should be taken, however, to avoid premature closure about what constitutes either improved measurement of psychopathology or improved procedures for combining scores on these measures into diagnoses. Much of the most intensive work on the development of new measuring instruments has focused mainly and, until very recently, exclusively on psychiatric patients, usually inpatients (for example, Endicott and Spitzer 1978; Wing, Cooper, and Sartorius 1974). There is no a priori guarantee that the resulting instruments will be suitable for epidemiologic investigations of general populations (cf. Dohrenwend et al. 1978). Any one of a variety of case-finding and classification procedures have been and can be used in epidemiologic research and the users will tend to testify that the procedures have "worked." Such testimony, however, will be no better guides to adequacy in the future than they have been in the past unless the testimony is based on rigorous evidence of reliability and validity. What is needed is something between anarchy and orthodoxy where case identification and classification are concerned. The "something" required might be called a disciplined competition where the rules are spelled out and where the weight of the evidence for reliability and validity decides the outcome (for example, Dohrenwend and Shrout, in press). Such programs of methodological research, however, would be difficult, time consuming, and expensive. There is little provision for them under current policies of granting agencies. It is difficult to see, however, how the field can advance without them.

Few would argue about the importance of a solid contribution from psychiatric epidemiology to the knowledge base for assessing the current state of affairs and planning the future of mental health efforts in this country. With all its imperfections, this specialty even now has the firmest (in fact, the only) answers available on a number of the most important questions the President's Commission on Mental Health was concerned with. It could do a great deal more.

NOTE

1. B. P. Dohrenwend, P. E. Shrout, G. Egri, and F. S. Mendelsohn. What psychiatric screening scales measure in the general population. Part 2. The components of demoralization by contrast with other dimensions of psychopathology. Submitted for publication. (Copies available from B. P. Dohrenwend, Social Psychiatry Research Unit, Columbia University, 100 Haven Avenue, New York, N.Y. 10032.)

REFERENCES

Dohrenwend, B. P., and Shrout, P. E. Toward the development of two-stage procedure for case identification and classification in psychiatric epidemiology. In R. G. Simmons (Ed.), *Research in Community and Mental Health* 2, Greenwich, Connecticut: JAI Press, in press.

Dohrenwend, B. P., Yager, T. J., Egri, G., and Mendelsohn, F. S. 1978. The psychiatric status schedule as a measure of dimensions of psychopathology in the general population. *Archives of General Psychiatry* 35: 731–7.

Endicott, J., and Spitzer, R. L. 1978. A diagnostic interview: the schedule for affective disorders and schizophrenia. *Archives of General Psychiatry* 35: 837–44.

Frank, J. D. 1973. *Persuasion and Healing*. Baltimore: Johns Hopkins University Press (originally published 1961).

Greenley, J. R., and Mechanic, D. 1976. Social selection in seeking help for psychological problems. *Journal of Health and Social Behavior* 17: 249–62.

Hollingshead, A. B., and Redlich, F. C. 1958. *Social Class and Mental Illness*. New York: Wiley.

Kramer, M. 1976. Issues in the development of statistical and epidemiological data for mental health services research. *Psychological Medicine* 6: 185–215.

Rabkin, J. 1975. The role of attitudes toward mental illness in evaluation of mental health programs. In M. Guttentag and E. L. Struening (Eds.), *Handbook of Evaluation Research*. Vol. 2. Beverly Hills, Calif.: Sage Publications.

Regier, D. A., Goldberg, I. D., and Tabue, C. A. 1978. The de facto U.S. mental health service system: a public health perspective. *Archives of General Psychiatry* 35: 685–93.

Task Force on Nomenclature and Statistics of the American Psychiatric Association. 1978. *Diagnostic and Statistical Manual of Mental Disorders*, 3rd ed., DSM-III Draft, 1st printing. Washington, D.C.: American Psychiatric Association.

Tischler, G. L., Henisz, J. E., Myers, J. K., and Boswell, P. C. 1975. Utilization of mental health services. 1. Patienthood and the prevalence of symptomatology in the community. *Archives of General Psychiatry* 32: 411–5.

Wing, J. K., Cooper, J. E., and Sartorius, N. 1974. *The Measurement and Classification of Psychiatric Symptoms*. London: Cambridge.

NAME INDEX

SUBJECT INDEX

adolescence, 17, 19, 23, 24

affective psychosis, 52, 151, 152; rates of, 52, 63, 67, 102; by sex, 54; U.S. and non-U.S. rates compared, 52

age, 15, 17–18, 23, 24, 150, 151; proportion of true cases in treatment, 138–39, 143

alcoholism, 5, 46, 58; rates of, 65, 67; by sex, 65; U.S. and non-U.S. rates compared, 65

American Indians, 47, 49; and alcoholism, 65 (*see also* Shore)

antisocial behavior, 5, 22–23

antisocial personality, 46, 55, 58, 64–65; rates of, 66–67

anxiety, generalized, 64, 101

arteriosclerotic psychoses, 96

autism, 18, 23

Baltimore study, 46–48, 97–102 (*see also* Pasamanick)

borderline features, 62

case finding, 4, 5, 45–46, 48, 50, 95–96; multimethod, multistage procedures, 11–17; parent informants, 11–15; screening, 13–15; teacher informants, 11–17; community informants, 46, 47–48, 50, 60, 134

Center for Epidemiological Studies Depression Scale CES-D, 117, 119

charge from the President's Commission, 1, 2, 4, 154, 155

classification, 4, 5; Diagnostic and Statistical Manual of Mental Disorders, 10, 62, 63, 64, 155; multiaxial system, 9; multivariate techniques, 10; World Health Organization (WHO) International Classification of Diseases, 9, 155; Research Diagnostic Criteria, 62–64, 65–66, 67, 101

clinical disorder, 124–26; relation to screening scales, 115; and demoralization, 126–27; estimate of proportion in treatment, 135, 147

clinical judgment, 13, 45–46, 153 (*see also* psychiatrists)

clinical maladjustment, 6, 10–18, 150, 152

cross-checks, 124–25, 152, 153

demoralization, 6, 115–27, 135, 151, 152, 153; defined, 115

depression: major, 63, 101; minor, 64, 101

Diagnostic and Statistical Manual of Mental Disorders of the American Psychiatric Association: DSM I, 64; DSM II, 64; DSM III, 10, 62, 63–64, 155

drug addiction, 5, 46, 58, 64; rates of, 65–67

ethnicity, 17–18, 150

etiology, 154, 155

Europe, 5

European and Canadian studies using clinical judgment, 49–50, 97

family structure, 17, 23

Florida study, 47 (*see also* Schwab)·

General Well Being Scale, 117, 119

geographic region, 17–18, 151

Gurin scale, 117

Health Opinion Survey (HOS), 117, 119, 125, 139

heroin use, rates of, 66

Hutterites, 47, 49–50, 133 (*see also* Eaton and Weil)

hyperkinesis, 19

incidence, 4

institutionalized cases, 46, 47–48, 55, 62–63, 65, 96–98, 104; elderly, 96, 101

IQ, 23

Langner 22 item index, 117, 119, 125–26, 139

learning disability, 19

manic depressive psychosis, 138

marital status and proportion of "true" cases in treatment, 138–39, 147, 148

measurement biases, 59–60

median rate, justification for its use, 51, 59–60

Midtown Manhattan Study, 133–34, 135

minimal brain dysfunction, 19

Monroe County, New York State, Psychiatric Register, 61
multiaxial system, 9–10
multimethod, multistage procedures, 11–17
multivariate techniques, 10

National Institute of Mental Health, 3
neuroses, 5, 151, 152, 154; narrow and broad definitions of, 64, 67–68; rates of, 52, 63–64, 67–68, 101–102, 103; by sex, 54–55, 104; by social class, 56–57; U.S. and non-U.S. rates compared, 52, 59, 63–64, 101
neurotic behavior, 23, 24
New Haven studies: of treated prevalence rates, 61; of true prevalence rates, 62–64, 65–66, 67, 99–102
New Jersey study, 47 (*see also* Trussell)
New York City studies, 46–47 (*see also* Srole, Washington Heights Manhattan study)

organic psychoses among the elderly, 96, 151; U.S. and European rates compared, 98–99; rates of, 98–99; by sex, 102 (*see also* senile psychoses, arteriosclerotic psychoses)

panic disorder, 64, 101
personality disorders, 5, 46, 151–52, 154; narrow and broad definitions, 64–65; rates of, 64–68, 101–2, 103–4; by sex, 54–55, 104; by social class, 58; U.S. and non-U.S. rates compared, 64
phobic disorder, 64, 101
President's Commission on Mental Health, 1, 3–4, 6–7, 154, 155, 156
prevalence defined, 7, 150, 155
preventive action, 154, 155
prognosis: antisocial behavior, 22–23; neuroses, 23–24; psychoses, 23
psychiatric diagnosis, 5–6; cross-national differences in criteria, 68; need for explicit rules of, 68
psychiatric disorders, functional, 3, 151, 152; rates of, 52, 55–56, 64–68, 101; by social class, 55; U.S. and non-U.S. rates compared, 52, 59–60 (*see also* affective psychosis, alcoholism, antisocial personality disorder, drug addiction, neu-

roses, psychoses, functional, schizophrenia)
psychiatric disorders, functional and organic, rates of, 98, 99 (*see also* affective psychosis, alcoholism, antisocial personality, drug addiction, neuroses, organic psychoses, personality disorder, psychiatric disorders, functional, psychoses, functional, schizophrenia)
psychiatric nomenclature, expansion following World War II, 45, 60, 64–65
Psychiatric Register (*see* Monroe County)
Psychoses: adolescence, 18–19, 23; childhood, 18, 23; proportion of cases in treatment, 135, 138–39, 147; rates of functional, 52, 99–101, 103–4; functional by sex, 52–55, 102, 104; functional by social class, 56; U.S. and non-U.S. rates of functional compared, 52, 59-60, 151 (*see also* affective psychosis, schizophrenia)
public attitudes, 154

reliability, 4, 9, 155, 156
Research Diagnostic Criteria, 62–64, 65, 67, 99–101

Salt Lake City study, 47, 48 (*see also* Cole)
San Francisco study, 98
schizophrenia, 5, 46, 151–152, 154; acute schizophrenic reaction, 61–62; borderline, 61–62; childhood, 18; narrow and broad definitions of, 67–68; proportion of cases in treatment, 135, 138, 147; rates of, 52, 60–63, 67–68, 101–2; by sex, 54–55; by social class, 56; U.S. and non-U.S. rates compared, 52
screening scales, 5, 6, 45, 114–19, 134; relation to clinical disorder, 115
senile psychoses, 96–97
sex, 6, 17, 18, 52–55, 152, 154; differences in rates of demoralization, 123–124; proportion of "true" cases in treatment, 138–39, 147 (*see also* affective psychosis, alcoholism, neuroses, organic psychoses, psychoses, schizophrenia)
situation-specificity, 13
social class, 6, 13, 17–18, 52, 55–58, 150, 152, 154; differences in rates of demoralization, 123–24; proportion of "true" cases in treatment, 138–39, 143, 147 (*see*

ABOUT THE AUTHORS

DR. BRUCE P. DOHRENWEND is Foundations' Fund for Research in Psychiatry Professor in the College of Physicians and Surgeons of Columbia University. He received his B.A. from Columbia College, his M.A. from Columbia University, and his Ph.D. in social psychology from Cornell University. Dr. Dohrenwend is Director of Columbia's Research Training Program in Psychiatric Epidemiology supported by the National Institute of Mental Health, and Principal Investigator on two NIMH research grants in the field of psychiatric epidemiology. He holds a Research Scientist Award from that Institute. Coauthor with Dr. Barbara Snell Dohrenwend of *Social Status and Psychological Disorder,* and coeditor with her of *Stressful Life Events: Their Nature and Effects.* Dr. Dohrenwend has also published many articles in leading journals in the fields of psychology, psychiatry, and sociology.

DR. BARBARA SNELL DOHRENWEND is Professor and Head of the Division of Sociomedical Sciences in the School of Public Health, Columbia University. She received her B.A. from Wellesley College and her M.A. and Ph.D. in Psychology from Columbia University. She is coauthor with Dr. Bruce Dohrenwend of *Social Status and Psychological Disorder* and coeditor with him of *Stressful Life Events,* and has published many articles in major journals in psychology, sociology, and public opinion research. She is past president of the Division of Community Psychology of the American Psychological Association and currently chairs the Society for Life History Research in Psychopathology.

MS. MADELYN SCHWARTZ GOULD is a Fellow in the Psychiatric Epidemiology Training Program at Columbia University. She received her B.S., summa cum laude, in Psychology from Brooklyn College, her M.A. in Psychology from Princeton University, and her M.P.H. from Columbia University. She is currently a candidate for the Ph.D. in Epidemiology at Columbia University.

MR. BRUCE G. LINK is a Fellow in the Psychiatric Epidemiology Training Program at Columbia University. He received his B.A. from Earlham College, Richmond, Indiana, and his M.A. and M.Phil. in Sociology from Columbia University. He is currently a candidate for the Ph.D. in Sociology at Columbia.

DR. RICHARD NEUGEBAUER is currently a Research Scientist in epidemiology at New York State Department of Mental Hygiene, Psychiatric Institute and a Research Associate in the Gertrude H. Sergievsky Center in the faculty of Medicine at Columbia University, which is devoted to the study of the epidemiology of neurological disorders. After completing a Ph.D. in History at Columbia University in 1976, he received three years of postdoctoral training in psychiatric epidemiology funded by the National Institute of Mental Health. He has authored papers and articles in psychiatric and neurological epidemiology and on the history of mental illness.

MS. ROBIN WUNSCH-HITZIG is a Fellow in the Psychiatric Epidemiology Training Program at Columbia University. She received her B.A. from the University of Michigan in Social Work and her M.A. in Sociology from New York University. She is currently a candidate for the Ph.D. in Sociology at New York University. In addition to her academic specialty, psychiatric sociology, she has worked for ten years as a researcher. Eight of those ten years were spent studying the emotional problems of children.